MEETING
St. Luke
TODAY

MEETING

St. Luke

TODAY

Understanding the Man,
His Mission, and His Message

DANIEL J. HARRINGTON, SJ

LOYOLA PRESS.
A JESUIT MINISTRY
Chicago

LOYOLA PRESS.
A JESUIT MINISTRY

3441 N. Ashland Avenue
Chicago, Illinois 60657
(800) 621-1008
www.loyolapress.com

Cover design by Kathryn Seckman Kirsch
Interior design by Kathryn Seckman Kirsch and Joan Bledig

Library of Congress Cataloging-in-Publication Data
Harrington, Daniel J.
   Meeting St. Luke today / Daniel J. Harrington.
      p. cm.
   Includes bibliographical references (p.   ).
   ISBN-13: 978-0-8294-2916-9
   ISBN-10: 0-8294-2916-6
   1. Bible. N.T. Luke—Commentaries. 2. Bible. N.T. Luke—Criticism,
interpretation, etc. I. Title. II. Title: Meeting Saint Luke today.
   BS2595.53.H37 2009
   226.4'066—dc22
                                                    2009019118

Printed in the United States of America
09 10 11 12 13 14 Versa 10 9 8 7 6 5 4 3 2 1

Contents

Part Four: Luke's Gospel in Christian Life

A Year Dedicated to Luke the Evangelist

In the Year C (2010, 2013, 2016, 2019, 2022, etc.) of the Catholic Church's lectionary of Scripture readings for Mass, the Gospel passage almost every Sunday is taken from St. Luke. In the New Testament we meet the person we call St. Luke only indirectly. We do so primarily through the two books that have traditionally been ascribed to him: the Gospel according to Luke and the Acts of the Apostles. These two writings are among the longest and most influential books in the New Testament. Indeed, what we call Luke's Gospel is sometimes described as the most beautiful book ever written.

My hope is that this guide to Luke's Gospel may help those who teach, preach, meditate, pray, and discuss the Sunday Scripture readings and that it will open up some of the riches in this attractive and challenging text. I hope as well that this little book might be an entry point into the many treasures that God has given us in the Holy Bible.

After a brief introduction to what we can say with confidence about Luke the Evangelist, this volume provides in six chapters a narrative analysis of the entire Gospel of Luke. These chapters focus on the Gospel's words and images, characters, plot, literary forms, indications of time and place, and theological message. The next two chapters examine how Luke handed on and interpreted earlier traditions and how Luke developed key themes throughout his Gospel. The last two chapters suggest how a person might pray on the basis of Luke's texts by using the methods of *lectio divina* ("sacred reading") and Ignatian contemplation, and how in the Year C of the Sunday cycle of Gospel readings Luke's portrait of Jesus can challenge us to "go and do likewise" (Luke 10:37). Each chapter concludes with two or three questions for reflection and discussion.

I am grateful to Joseph Durepos for the invitation to write this book and to Loyola Press for continuing to promote the many different facets of Jesuit spirituality.

PART ONE

Meeting St. Luke

1

The Evangelist and His Gospel

In the main text of the Gospel of Luke, the author never identifies himself as Luke by name (as Paul does in his letters and as John does in Revelation). The title "According to Luke" seems to have been added later to the main text, sometime in the second century. From at least the second century on, the author of this Gospel has been identified as one of Paul's coworkers, named Luke.

The first verse in the Acts of the Apostles ("In the first book, Theophilus, I wrote about all that Jesus did") indicates that the same author wrote both Luke's Gospel and Acts. At several points in Acts (16:11–16; 20:5–16; 21:1–17; 27:1—28:16) the writer uses "we" language, suggesting that he accompanied Paul on his missionary journeys and on his way to Rome. In Paul's letters a person named Luke is described as one of Paul's "fellow workers" (Philemon 24), the "beloved physician" (Colossians 4:14), and Paul's faithful friend (2 Timothy 4:11). Christian tradition identifies this Luke as the Evangelist and as the author of two volumes: the Gospel of Luke and the Acts of the Apostles.

However close Luke's relationship to Paul may have been, it's important to recognize Luke's distinctive literary and theological

Since many have undertaken to set down an orderly account of the events that have been fulfilled among us, just as they were handed on to us by those who from the beginning were eyewitnesses and servants of the word, I too decided, after investigating everything carefully from the very first, to write an orderly account for you, most excellent Theophilus, so that you may know the truth concerning the things about which you have been instructed.

—Luke 1:1–4

approaches to Jesus and the movement he began. This is Luke's Gospel, not Paul's Gospel. A later tradition identifies Luke as a painter. While the history behind this identification is dubious, it makes the point that Luke is a master of details. Often, what is on the surface may seem straightforward and simple but emerges on further inspection to have hidden depth and complexity. Readers need to pay careful attention to the details because Luke's truth is often in the details.

The focus of this book is Luke's biography of Jesus, not the biography of Luke. In fact, we can say little about Luke's biography beyond the few mentions of someone named Luke in the Pauline letters and perhaps the "we" passages in Acts. But there are several things we can say with great certainty about the Evangelist who wrote Luke's Gospel. The Evangelist whom we call Luke knew the Greek language very well and was capable of writing it in various literary styles. While probably a non-Jew (a Gentile) by birth, the author of Luke-Acts certainly knew a great deal about the Jewish Scriptures, may have been a "God fearer" (a Gentile associate member of a Jewish synagogue), became a Christian perhaps under Paul's influence, and believed that the Jewish Scriptures were being fulfilled in Jesus and the early Christian movement.

The original audience for which Luke wrote was most likely made up mainly of Gentile Christians. However, in order to understand this Gospel they would have to have known a good deal about Judaism and the Jewish Scriptures. Perhaps they too were God fearers, that is, non-Jews attracted to Judaism by its monotheism, high ethical standards, and rich community life.

There is little consensus about exactly where Luke wrote his Gospel. While earlier scholars placed it in Antioch in Syria or Caesarea in Palestine, now there is a tendency to locate it in Greece or even Rome. Wherever it originated, it soon became a Gospel for all the churches and enjoyed wide circulation throughout the ancient Mediterranean world.

At several points in this Gospel (19:43–44; 21:20, 24) the Evangelist seems to refer to the destruction of Jerusalem in AD 70, and his use of Mark's Gospel as a source suggests that he composed his Gospel around AD 85 or 90 on the basis of earlier traditions. Luke's account of the spread of the gospel in Acts breaks off rather abruptly around AD 60 with Paul still exercising his ministry of the word while under house arrest in Rome. Luke, however, seems to have completed his two-volume work about twenty-five or thirty years later. Whether he intended a third volume or was satisfied with telling only the story of the earliest years of the Christian movement is debated among scholars.

With regard to the origin and purpose of Luke's Gospel, we are on firmer ground when we focus on the Evangelist's own words in 1:1–4. This is the kind of statement that historians in antiquity customarily placed at the beginning of their works. Written in an elegant classical Greek style, the preface to Luke's Gospel is one long sentence in the original text.

Luke 1:1–4

Since many have undertaken to set down an orderly account of the events that have been fulfilled among us, just as they were handed on to us by those who

from the beginning were eyewitnesses and servants
of the word, I too decided, after investigating everything carefully from the very first, to write an orderly
account for you, most excellent Theophilus, so that
you may know the truth concerning the things about
which you have been instructed.

In his preface Luke refers to "many" previous writers on the
topic of Jesus and proposes to write an "orderly account" as they
did. His subject matter is "the events that have been fulfilled
among us"—certainly Jesus' birth, public ministry, passion and
death, and resurrection, as well as the spread of the early church
throughout the Mediterranean world, as described in Acts. Luke
claims to have relied on trustworthy sources ("eyewitnesses and
servants of the word") and to have carried out extensive research
("investigating everything carefully from the very first"). He does
not claim that he himself was an eyewitness to Jesus. He dedi-
cates his book to "Theophilus." Writers in antiquity often relied
on the generosity of a wealthy patron for financial support. The
name means "lover of God." This may have been his real name or
a nickname honoring his piety. Or it may be merely a symbol for
all of Luke's prospective readers.

The Evangelist's basic purpose was to provide Theophilus
and other readers with an "orderly account." It is important we
understand that this expression does not necessarily mean orderly
only in the matter of accurate chronology. It more likely means
arranging the episodes and teachings in a way that best achieves
the desired effect on the reader. What Luke hoped is that his

narrative about Jesus would provide Theophilus with greater information and certainty about what he had already learned about Jesus in his earlier instruction. The second book in Luke's two-volume work—the Acts of the Apostles—is also dedicated to Theophilus and concerns the spread of the good news about Jesus from Jerusalem to Rome.

One of the written sources that Luke used was Mark's Gospel, and so his Gospel (as well as Matthew's) can be regarded as a revised and expanded version of Mark. Luke improved Mark's Greek, tightened and polished Mark's narrative, and included source material apparently not available to Mark. He used Mark's Gospel in three large blocks (Luke 3:1—6:19; 8:4—9:50; 18:15—24:11). In between there are two large blocks of non-Marcan material: what scholars call the "small insertion" (Luke 6:20—8:3) and the "large insertion" (9:51—18:14).

Another source that Luke used was the collection of sayings attributed to Jesus that is known today as the Sayings Source "Q." The symbol Q derives from the German word for "source" (*Quelle*). Matthew also used Q, though independently from Luke. Most of the Q material appears in the two "insertions." Almost half of Luke's Gospel (including the infancy narrative and several of the parables, such as the Good Samaritan and the prodigal son) consists of special material found only in Luke's Gospel and so is designated by the symbol "L" (for Luke). The L material was probably not a single book but rather a combination of traditional written and oral materials along with some passages composed by the Evangelist himself.

Luke set out to compose an orderly account about Jesus' birth, public activity, passion and death, and resurrection on the basis of traditional materials in order to inspire greater certainty and confidence in his readers concerning their Christian faith. To its first readers it would have looked like a biography in which Jesus of Nazareth appears as the exemplary figure (though Jesus as the Son of God is far more than just a good example).

Luke's narrative begins by placing Jesus' birth and his preparation for his public ministry in the context of the faithful within Israel and the Jewish Scriptures (1:5—4:13). Then he describes Jesus' public ministry in three phases: his early activities in Galilee (4:14—9:50), his journey with his disciples from Galilee to Jerusalem (9:51—19:27), and his ministry in Jerusalem (19:28—21:38). Finally he discusses Jesus' passion, death, and resurrection in Jerusalem (22:1—24:53). In this geographical-theological organization Luke followed Mark's outline. But he has added an infancy narrative, greatly expanded the journey narrative from two and half to ten chapters, and included accounts of the risen Jesus' appearances to his followers.

In telling his story of Jesus, Luke develops several themes that carry through not only in the Gospel but also into Acts. He discerns three phases in salvation history: from Adam to John the Baptist, the time of Jesus as the center of history, and the age of the Holy Spirit and the church. He places Jesus in the context of world history, while emphasizing Jesus' integrity and political innocence. He portrays Jesus as showing special concern for the poor and other marginal persons, as praying at the most important moments in his life, as a prophet sent from God, as the best example of his own teachings, and as a model for Christians facing persecution and martyrdom.

In reading and praying over Luke's Gospel it is important to approach the text as one of the principal witnesses to the life and teachings of Jesus of Nazareth, the one whom early Christians recognized as the Son of God and the Lord Jesus Christ. At the same time we need to appreciate (following what Luke says in 1:1–4) that this Gospel is the product of a long and complex process of transmission from Jesus (AD 30 or so) through the early church to the Evangelist (AD 85–90), and we can expect to find new contributions and adaptations at each point along the way. Moreover, in interpreting Luke's Gospel we need to respect the literary forms and conventions that the Evangelist chose to use, and the meaning that he intended to express. In this way we will read Luke in accord with what the Second Vatican Council said about the Bible and its interpretation in its 1965 Dogmatic Constitution on Divine Revelation (*Dei verbum*).

For Reflection and Discussion

From the author's preface in Luke 1:1–4, what do you expect from reading and studying this Gospel?

What might Luke have meant when he described his goal as providing an "orderly account"?

PART TWO

Luke's Story of Jesus

2

The Time of Preparation

Luke 1:1—4:13

Luke wrote a narrative about Jesus. He could have produced a collection of Jesus' wise sayings (like the Sayings Source Q) or a theological treatise on the significance of Jesus' life, death, and resurrection (like Romans and Hebrews). Instead he decided to tell the story of Jesus from his birth to his death and resurrection in the form of an orderly narrative.

In Luke's narrative Jesus is the central character, and all the other characters relate to him, either positively or negatively. The plot traces the story of Jesus from his birth and preparation, through his public ministry first in Galilee, then on the road, and finally in Jerusalem, where he meets his death and experiences his resurrection. All this happens when Israel is part of the Roman Empire and under Roman control. Place and time are clearly important elements in the plot. Luke tells his story from the perspective of a believer in Jesus (as the Messiah, Son of Man, Son of God, Lord, etc.) and in light of what he describes in his preface as serious research. While not claiming to be an eyewitness himself,

As the people were filled with expectation, and all were questioning in their hearts concerning John, whether he might be the Messiah, John answered all of them by saying, "I baptize you with water; but one who is more powerful than I is coming; I am not worthy to untie the thong of his sandals. He will baptize you with the Holy Spirit and fire."

—Luke 3:15–16

he presents himself as an all-knowing narrator whose words can be trusted.

One approach to studying the Gospels that has become popular in recent years is called narrative analysis. This approach pays special attention to the text as it has come down to us in the Bible, that is, to the "text in front of us" rather than to what may be behind the text or what we might want to make the text say. It focuses on characterization, plot, time and place, the narrator's point of view, and so on. The six chapters in this section provide a brief narrative analysis of Luke's Gospel. While not a substitute for reading the text, it is intended as a help or guide to reading Luke's Gospel in a fresh way and discovering why Luke's Gospel may well be the most beautiful book ever written.

An important function of Luke's preface (1:1–4) is to establish the reliability of the author and to delineate the ideal reader. The author tells us that he has done serious research on the topic and has set out to write an orderly account that will be both informative and persuasive. His ideal reader is Theophilus, a "lover of God," who has already received some instruction about Jesus and the early days of Christianity. The Gospel will attempt to provide Theophilus (and all readers) with even greater certainty about these matters.

The first section of Luke's Gospel concerns the circumstances of Jesus' birth (1:5—2:52) and his adult life before his public ministry (3:1—4:13). It tells us who Jesus is and why he is so important. Luke prepares us as readers to understand that from the very beginning of his life on earth Jesus was no ordinary person. Rather, by his origins and early experiences, Jesus was well qualified to appear on the public stage as a wise teacher, powerful healer, and faithful witness to God as his Father.

In Luke's **infancy narrative** (1:5—2:52) there is a remarkable shift in literary style from the elegant classical Greek of the preface (1:1–4) to the Semitic style of the Greek version of the Hebrew Scriptures (the Septuagint). With this change in style, Luke places us readers in the world of the Old Testament, and he signals that Jesus' birth took place among the best representatives of the people of God. The Word became flesh in a particular place and time: in the land of Israel under the Roman Empire in what we have come to call the first century.

The structure of Luke's infancy narrative promotes a comparison between John the Baptist and Jesus. The point is that while John is great, Jesus is even greater. This comparison is carried out first in the announcements of the births of John (1:5–25) and of Jesus (1:26–38) and then in the descriptions of the births of John (1:57–80) and of Jesus (2:1–40). The comparison is reinforced in the episodes of the visitation (1:39–56) and of the child Jesus in the temple (2:41–52), as well as in the hymns proclaimed by Mary (the Magnificat in 1:46–55) and Zechariah (the Benedictus in 1:68–79). Luke's infancy narrative begins and ends in the Jerusalem temple and moves around the land of Israel with stops at Nazareth in Galilee, the hill country of Judea, Bethlehem, the Jerusalem temple twice again, and back to Nazareth.

In **the announcement of John's birth** (1:5–25), the main character is Zechariah, an elderly priest taking his turn serving at the Jerusalem temple. To him the angel Gabriel announces the birth of John the Baptist and his mission to prepare God's people to turn to the Lord their God. Zechariah's encounter with the angel in 1:11–20 follows a pattern that will be replicated in the announcement of Jesus' birth to Mary: commission (to be John's father), objection (we're too old), reassurance (from Gabriel), and sign (his being silenced). Zechariah's being struck mute provides the sign, and so his wife, Elizabeth, becomes pregnant. While this episode contains several motifs that will be developed throughout the Gospel narrative (prayer, joy, the Holy Spirit), the most obvious theme is that the story of salvation begins at Jerusalem, in the temple. At the close of the Gospel, the risen Jesus will commission his disciples to bring the good news to all nations, "beginning from Jerusalem" (24:47).

In **the announcement of Jesus' birth** (1:26–38), the main character is Mary, a young woman of Nazareth who is engaged to Joseph. Her encounter with Gabriel proceeds according to a similar pattern: commission (to be the mother of the Son of the Most High), objection (I am a virgin), reassurance (the Holy Spirit will come upon you), and sign (Elizabeth's pregnancy). While John is to be the prophet like Elijah preparing God's people, Jesus will be the Son of God and the Davidic Messiah whose rule will last forever. Thus John is great, but Jesus is even greater. While Zechariah seems puzzled by his commission, Mary, once she understands, embraces her task enthusiastically, "Here am I, the servant of the Lord; let it be with me according to your word" (1:38). While John's conception takes place in the usual human way, in the case of Jesus the Holy Spirit is active in his life from its very beginning.

In **the Visitation** (1:39–56), the two expectant mothers—Elizabeth and Mary—come together in a way that further establishes the superiority of Jesus. Under the power of the Holy Spirit, Elizabeth (the older woman) declares Mary "blessed" and refers to her as "the mother of my Lord." Even John in his mother's womb rejoices to be in the presence of Mary and Jesus. Mary is also declared "blessed" because of her trust in God's word to her (see 1:38; 2:19). Mary's song of praise (the Magnificat, 1:46–55) celebrates God's practice of choosing lowly instruments (like herself) and turning the natural order of society upside down in fulfilling his promises to his people. Mary then leaves Judea and returns to Nazareth in Galilee (1:56).

At the **birth and naming of John** (1:57–80) there is great joy in the hill country of Judea at Elizabeth having borne a son and at the perfect agreement regarding his name (which means "the Lord shows mercy") in accord with the angel's words in 1:13–14. Zechariah's hymn of celebration (the Benedictus, 1:68–79) highlights the themes of salvation, divine mercy, and covenant. Yet the focus of his praise is mainly Jesus the Son of David, while he relegates his own son, John, to the role of prophet and precursor—Zechariah, too, gives witness to the superiority of Jesus. According to 1:80, when John grew up, he went off to the Judean Desert until his appearance as an adult on the public stage (in 3:1–20).

Luke's account of **Jesus' birth and naming** (2:1–21) first explains how Jesus came to be born in Bethlehem, the city of David his ancestor. Joseph and Mary had to travel there to be enrolled in an imperial census (2:1–5). The birth of Jesus (2:6–7) takes place in humble circumstances. The child is placed in a manger (a trough from which animals ate) because there was no room in the inn. Nevertheless, Jesus' birth is celebrated by an angelic proclamation and chorus (2:8–14), and the shepherds (lowly figures in their society) make a respectful visit to the parents and their child (2:15–20). The contrast between the nobility of the child Jesus and the humble circumstances of his birth is brought out especially in the angelic identification of him, "to you is born this day in the city of David a Savior, who is the Messiah, the Lord" (2:11). The naming of Jesus (in 2:21) fulfills the angel's prophecy in 1:31. His name means "the Lord saves."

Forty days after Jesus' birth, the family travels to the Jerusalem temple for the purification of Mary after childbirth and for the **presentation of the child Jesus** (2:22–40). There two elderly representatives of the best in biblical piety—Simeon and Anna—recognize the true nature and destiny of this child. Using the language of Isaiah, Simeon hails Jesus as "a light for revelation to the Gentiles and for glory to your people Israel" (2:32), while also introducing the possibility of eventual suffering for the child and his mother, thus pointing forward to the Passion. Anna also recognizes this child as God's instrument of Jerusalem's redemption.

At the age of twelve, **Jesus accompanies his parents on a pilgrimage at Passover to the Jerusalem temple** (2:41–52). There Jesus debates with the great scholars and wins their admiration for his brilliance. His parents, however, are surprised at his behavior in separating himself from them, and they fail to understand it. Jesus' explanation ("Did you not know that I must be in my Father's house?" [2:49]) establishes God as his real father and the Jerusalem temple as his real home. Thus Luke's infancy narrative ends where it began, and the family goes back to Nazareth.

From his account of Jesus' birth, Luke moves the narrative abruptly forward to **John and Jesus as adults** in 3:1–20, all the while reinforcing the superiority of Jesus. The list of rulers in 3:1–2 situates them both in the context of history in the Mediterranean world around AD 29. The extended quotation of Isaiah 40 serves to identify Jesus as the Lord and John as his herald and highlights Jesus as the one who brings "the salvation of God." The sample of John's preaching in 3:7–14 consists of warnings about the judgment accompanying the coming of God's kingdom and instructions on how to act in the face of it. In 3:15–18 John admits that his baptism in water is no match for Jesus' baptism in "the Holy Spirit and fire." In a peculiar move Luke in 3:19–20 describes John's arrest and imprisonment for criticizing Herod Antipas before his account of the baptism of Jesus, thus leaving unclear who exactly baptized Jesus. For Luke, John belongs to the time of Israel (see 16:16), whereas Jesus represents a new period in salvation history, the center of time.

The remaining three passages in Luke's account of the time of preparation concern various aspects of **Jesus' identity as the Son of God**. The revelation of Jesus as God's Son (3:21–22) occurs after his baptism and while he is at prayer. A voice from the heavens declares, "You are my Son, the Beloved; with you I am well pleased." The genealogy of Jesus in 3:23–38 traces his lineage back to "Adam son of God," thus emphasizing his universal significance for humankind. And the three tests or "temptations" in 4:1–13 establish what kind of Son of God Jesus really is. He is concerned with doing his Father's will as revealed in the Scriptures, not with physical pleasure, political power, and fame.

He passes the tests that ancient Israel in the wilderness failed, and he does so with quotations from the book of Deuteronomy.

Reflection and Discussion

How does Luke's infancy narrative prepare us for his story about Jesus as an adult?

How has this exploration into Luke's texts added to your thoughts and impressions about Jesus' relationship with John the Baptist?

3

Jesus' Ministry in Galilee

Luke 4:14—9:50

The first phase of Jesus' public ministry takes place around AD 30, in Galilee, which is the northern part of the land belonging to the Israelites. While Nazareth was where Jesus grew up, Capernaum serves as his home base as he and his followers move around the area. In this section Luke provides samples of Jesus' wise teachings and acts of power, while revealing who Jesus is and showing how some in Israel accept him and others reject him. Jesus is the central character throughout, and others react to him either positively or negatively. In this section Luke supplements passages from Mark with material from the Sayings Source Q and his own special sources (L).

Having been baptized in the Jordan River and tested in the Judean desert, Jesus in 4:14–15 returns to his home area in Galilee. Now he is "filled with the power of the Spirit," as if all the energy of the Spirit is concentrated in him.

In 4:16–30 Luke moves up and greatly expands Mark's episode of **Jesus' rejection in the synagogue at Nazareth** (see

[Jesus] came down with them and stood on a level place, with a great crowd of his disciples and a great multitude of people from all Judea, Jerusalem, and the coast of Tyre and Sidon. They had come to hear him and to be healed of their diseases; and those who were troubled with unclean spirits were cured. And all in the crowd were trying to touch him, for power came out from him and healed all of them.

—Luke 6:17–19

Mark 6:1–6). He uses the occasion to preview many of the themes he will develop as the narrative proceeds. The quotation from Isaiah 61 (and 58) describes perfectly who Jesus is and what he will do. He is the unique bearer of the Holy Spirit and the Anointed One who will bring God's good news, freedom, and healing to the oppressed. Jesus' sermon also introduces the notion of "today" as his special time and indeed the decisive moment in salvation history. The initial amazement of the crowd, however, soon turns into skepticism, selfishness, and hostility—a reaction to be repeated throughout the Gospel and Acts. Jesus acknowledges that it is the fate of prophets like himself to be rejected. Nevertheless, he defends the universal scope of his mission by appealing to the examples of the great biblical prophets, Elijah and Elisha, who ministered to Gentiles.

Using material from Mark 1:21–39, Luke in 4:31–44 shows that **Jesus was both a powerful healer and a faithful preacher of "the good news of the kingdom of God."** The fact that the demons recognize Jesus as the Holy One of God, the Son of God, and the Messiah indicates that his healing and teaching activities are part of a larger struggle against the forces of Satan.

Luke moves **the call of the first disciples** to 5:1–11 in order to give them some firsthand experience of Jesus as a teacher and miracle worker, and so makes more reasonable why Peter and others left everything and became followers of Jesus. Peter heard Jesus preaching from his boat and witnessed a miraculous catch of fish (see John 21:1–14). Thus Peter and his colleagues respond positively to Jesus' call to join him in his life-giving ministry as fishers of people.

The theme of Jesus as powerful in deed and word is carried forward in 5:12—6:11 with Luke's adaptation of material from Mark 1:40—3:6. Here **Jesus heals a leper and a paralyzed man, calls Levi the tax collector to become a disciple, answers questions about fasting and Sabbath observance, and heals a man with a withered hand on the Sabbath.** Luke notes at the beginning Jesus' practice of prayer (5:16) and at the end the growing hostility that Jesus meets (6:11).

For Luke, **the choosing of the twelve apostles** (6:12–16) is important because they will be principles of continuity between his Gospel and Acts. The momentous character of their appointment is highlighted by the notice that Jesus did so only after a long period of prayer.

For his first great speech, Jesus in 6:17–19 meets the crowd on a "level place." The audience approaches Jesus from many directions in the hope of experiencing the power of his word and healing action. Based on Jesus' sayings collected in the Sayings Source Q, **the Sermon on the Plain** (6:20–49) is Luke's equivalent of Matthew's Sermon on the Mount (Matthew 5:1—7:29).

In **the Beatitudes** (6:20–23) that begin the Sermon on the Plain, Jesus declares happy or fortunate some surprising persons (the poor, the hungry, the weeping, the persecuted) and then in 6:24–26 declares unhappy or even cursed some equally surprising persons (the rich, the full, the laughing, the famous). In the core of the sermon (6:27–38) Jesus teaches about love of enemies, offers four extreme examples of what that might mean, and gives as reason for doing so the Golden Rule (treat others as you wish them to treat you) and imitation of God's example in loving all his creatures (even those who are hostile to him). In 6:39–49, Jesus concludes by warning against hypocrisy and false teachers, insisting on good persons doing good deeds, and urging his listeners to build their lives on the solid foundation of his teaching.

The power of Jesus' word expressed in the Sermon on the Plain is reinforced by two miracle stories. In **healing the centurion's servant** (7:1–10), Jesus does so at a distance and by word alone. The Gentile centurion approaches Jesus through his Jewish friends and expresses trust in Jesus' power to heal. He recognizes Jesus' superior authority and his own unworthiness. In **restoring to life the son of the widow of Nain** (7:11–17), Jesus merely issues a verbal command ("Young man, I say to you, rise!") and the boy is immediately restored to life. The onlookers correctly identify Jesus as a prophet powerful in word and deed, and they discern in his action a divine visitation.

The relationship between John the Baptist and Jesus, which was a major topic in the infancy narrative, is taken up again in 7:18–35. When John inquires (presumably from prison; see 3:19–20) whether Jesus is "the one who is to come," Jesus responds in terms of what he has done in a way that echoes Isaiah 35:5–6 and 61:1—he performs the works of the Messiah. The departure of John's messengers leads into Jesus' own reflections on John's identity and on how both he and John are rejected by many of their contemporaries. Jesus identifies John as "more than a prophet." Nevertheless, John belongs to the time of Israel, whereas by his words and deeds Jesus has inaugurated the new time of God's kingdom. However, both John and Jesus have greater success with marginal persons in their society than with the religious and intellectual elites. Jesus compares their opponents to fickle children who refuse to play either sad games (with John) or happy games (with Jesus).

The charge that **Jesus is a friend of tax collectors and sinners** provides the occasion for the story of Simon the Pharisee and the sinful woman in 7:36–50. On the scale of religious observance and public reputation the two characters are opposites, yet the woman behaves in a grateful and loving manner toward Jesus (who apparently had forgiven her sins) while Simon grumbles that Jesus could not be a prophet if he allowed such a sinful woman to touch him. Rather than confronting Simon directly, Jesus in 7:40–43 first tells a parable about two debtors and elicits from Simon the admission that the debtor with the larger debt would be the more grateful of the two when the debts were forgiven. Then Jesus applies the parables to the two contrasting characters. The sinful woman whose great sins had been forgiven expresses her love on a grand scale, whereas Simon barely goes through the motions in offering Jesus the customary hospitality. The episode emphasizes that love of God (and Jesus) and forgiveness of sins cannot be separated.

The list of women who accompany Jesus (8:1–3) is a reminder that Jesus' first followers included more than the twelve apostles. Although historically, many people have identified Mary Magdalene with the sinful woman of 7:36–50, there is no scholarly evidence of this. These women will be witnesses to Jesus' wise teachings and powerful healings as well as to his death, burial, and empty tomb.

The material in 8:4—9:50 follows the outline found in Mark 4:1—6:44 and 8:27—9:41. The major topics are revelation and misunderstanding. **The parable of the sower and its interpretation** (8:4–15) explains why not every one of Jesus' contemporaries accepts his message, and the parable emphasizes the extraordinary results that the seed sown in good soil produces. Despite the refusal of many, the truth of Jesus words' shines more brightly than a lamp does in the dark (8:16–18), and the real family of Jesus is made up of those who "hear the word of God and do it" (8:19–21).

The displays of Jesus' power over the stormy sea, the demons, disease, and death in 8:22–56 (see Mark 4:35—5:43) make the widespread rejection of him even more puzzling. In stilling the storm Jesus does what only God can do according to the Old Testament (see, for example, Job 38:8–11; Psalms 74:13–17; 89:8–13). In exorcising the demons at Gerasa, Jesus continues his mission of breaking down Satan's power. In healing the woman with the flow of blood and restoring Jairus's daughter to life, Jesus acts as both the healer and the one who gives life and conquers death. These episodes depict Jesus as doing what God does, thus suggesting his divine status.

In **sending the twelve apostles (9:1–6) on a mission**, Jesus insists that they follow a simple lifestyle and keep their focus on proclaiming God's kingdom and healing the sick. Thus they do what Jesus does. After noting Herod Antipas's puzzlement over Jesus and the execution of John the Baptist (9:7–9), there comes the **feeding of the 5,000** (9:10–17), which connects with other banquet scenes in the Gospel and points forward to the Last Supper (22:14–20) and "the breaking of bread" in Acts (and the church's Eucharist).

Following the "great omission" of Mark 6:45—8:26, the Lucan narrative in 9:18–50 adapts Mark 8:27—9:41. The importance of **the first Passion prediction** (9:18–27) is signaled by the introductory mention of Jesus at prayer. While Peter correctly identifies Jesus as the Messiah, he recoils at the idea of a suffering Messiah and has to be instructed about the mystery of the cross.

The Transfiguration (9:28–36) takes place while Jesus is at prayer and provides a reminder about Jesus' identity as the Son of God (see 3:22) before he begins his journey to Jerusalem, which will lead to his passion, death, and resurrection. The disciples' failure to understand Jesus properly is underscored in a series of episodes: their inability to heal the boy with a demon (9:37–43), their failure to understand Jesus' second Passion prediction (9:44–45), their argument about who was the greatest among them (9:46–48), and their objection to the strange exorcist (9:49–50). Thus they show how much they (and we) need the instructions that Jesus will provide along the way to Jerusalem.

For Reflection and Discussion

In what sense is Jesus both a prophet and more than a prophet during his ministry in Galilee?

What is your favorite aspect of Jesus' Galilean ministry, and why?

Given what this chapter reveals about Luke's and others' accounts of the Sermon on the Plain (or Sermon on the Mount), how do you understand these teachings?

4

Jesus' Journey to Jerusalem, Part 1

9:51—13:30

The central part of Luke's Gospel (9:51—19:27) describes the journey of Jesus and his disciples from Galilee to Jerusalem. While taking over the idea from the journey narrative in Mark 8:22—10:52, Luke greatly expanded it and made it into a vehicle for including many other traditions from the Sayings Source Q and his special sources (L). The two major themes are the identity of Jesus (Christology) and what it means to follow him (discipleship).

Jesus comes from the mountain where the Transfiguration took place and goes to the border of Samaria. He returns to Galilee and continues his ministry in the context of a journey there. He eventually arrives in Judea and comes by way of Jericho to the Jerusalem temple. Luke envisions the journey as spread over a fairly long period and reinforces the notion of the journey with many references to it (9:52, 59; 10:1, 38; 13:22, 31–33; 14:25;

17:11; 18:31, 35; 19:1, 11, 28–29, 37). The journey's destination is Jerusalem, the place where prophets die (13:31–33).

According to 9:51–56, **Jesus expected the fate that awaited him in Jerusalem and nonetheless willingly embarked on his journey.** Early in the journey he and his messengers meet opposition from some Samaritans because they know that his destination is Jerusalem and not their sacred shrine at Shechem in Samaria. Also, he faces misunderstanding from his own disciples, who expect him to bring down fire upon those who oppose him, after the pattern set by the prophet Elijah in 2 Kings 1:9–12. According to 9:57–62, his disciples (and the readers) need to face up to the demands involved in following Jesus and to subordinate their own stability and even family obligations to the supreme importance of the kingdom of God.

The sending of the seventy (or seventy-two) disciples in 10:1–16 echoes the sending of the twelve apostles in 9:1–6. As Jesus' mission expands, the focus on the kingdom of God and a simple lifestyle remain central. In Jesus' time religions and philosophies were spread mainly by traveling missionaries, and so the sight of Jesus' followers extending his mission would not have been surprising. He warns prospective disciples to expect rejection and tells them how to deal with it nonviolently. Just as Jesus was rejected in cities in Galilee (Bethsaida, Chorazin, Capernaum), so his followers can expect the same treatment. As it was with the teacher, so it will be with the disciples.

On the disciples' return (10:17–24), they declare that demons have submitted to them as they performed exorcisms in Jesus' name. In response, Jesus first in 10:18–20 places their success in the context of his own mission of breaking down the power of Satan. Then with a prayer of thanksgiving in 10:21–22 Jesus notes his own success not with the wise and educated but rather with marginal persons ("infants"), and in 10:23–24 he declares blessed those who have been privileged to witness what his disciples are seeing in the time of Jesus, which is the middle or center of salvation history.

The three passages in 10:25—11:13 deal with different aspects of love: love of neighbor and love of God. The occasion is **Jesus' dialogue with a lawyer** in 10:25–28. When the lawyer asks how he might inherit eternal life, Jesus leads him to answer his own question and to join the two great biblical love commands: love of God (Deuteronomy 6:4–5) and love of neighbor (Leviticus 19:18).

The lawyer, however, cannot resist asking in 10:29, "And who is my neighbor?" Jesus responds with **the parable of the Good Samaritan**. In fact, the central character in the parable is a man who was robbed, beaten, and left for dead. The other characters all relate to him. In this situation the man's neighbor would be anyone willing to help him. That he was going down from Jerusalem to Jericho suggests that he might have been returning from a pilgrimage to the temple. That makes it all the more ironic that he would be passed and ignored first by a Jewish priest and then by a Levite, both members of the Jewish clerical class. What is even more surprising is that the one who finally helps him is not a Judean layman (as one might expect) but rather a Samaritan who not only tends to the man's wounds but also brings him to an inn and agrees to pay his expenses. In 10:36–37 Jesus returns to

Do not be afraid, little flock, for it is your Father's good pleasure to give you the kingdom. Sell your possessions, and give alms. Make purses for yourselves that do not wear out, an unfailing treasure in heaven, where no thief comes near and no mother destroys. For where your treasure is, there your heart will be also.

—Luke 12:32–34

the dialogue and elicits from the lawyer the answer that whoever helped the wounded man (even if the helper was a Samaritan) proved to be his neighbor. Jesus in turn challenges the lawyer (and us) to imitate the Good Samaritan's example: "go and do likewise."

According to 10:38–42, **two sisters named Mary and Martha welcomed Jesus into their home and offered him their hospitality.** Relying on the kindness of others was not unusual for traveling missionaries, including Jesus and his followers (see 9:3–4; 10:7). What was unusual was that a woman like Mary should join with the local men in listening to the teachings of Jesus. When Martha complains that Mary is neglecting the tasks that women normally performed (hospitality, household chores), Jesus defends Mary on the grounds that she has chosen "the better part" by listening to Jesus, and he challenges Martha to rethink her own priorities. Love of neighbor (shown by Martha) is important. But love of God (shown by Mary) is even more important.

Prayer is part of loving God. In 11:1–13 **Jesus offers a sample prayer and various teachings about persistence in our prayers for help.** It's important to note that this passage begins with Jesus at prayer. The sample prayer is Luke's version of what we call the Lord's Prayer. After addressing God simply as "Father," it provides two "you" petitions ("hallowed be your name. Your kingdom come") about the full coming of God's kingdom and three "we" petitions asking for sustenance, forgiveness, and protection in the coming period of testing. The parable of the friend at midnight (11:5–8) advocates a surprising boldness and persistence in prayer. And the sayings about the prayer of petition in 11:9–13 present the reason for such boldness and persistence: God truly wants to answer our prayers and to give us the gift of the Holy Spirit.

In 11:14–36 **Jesus makes clear that he is on God's side and not on Satan's side**. His casting out a mute demon in 11:14 provides the occasion for a debate between Jesus and his opponents about the source of his healing power. Is it from God or Satan? With a series of short parables, Jesus shows that he is on God's side in this battle and that attributing his power to Satan is a serious mistake in theological reasoning. Especially important is his saying in 11:20: "But if it is by the finger of God that I cast out the demons, then the kingdom of God has come to you." In other words, Jesus' healings are not spectacular displays designed only to draw attention to himself, but rather they are signs of the presence of God's kingdom in Jesus' ministry and previews of the fullness of God's kingdom yet to come. Nevertheless, though Satan's power may be weakened and even broken, it has not been utterly destroyed as the parable in 11:24–26 suggests.

In this context **the true disciple of Jesus is described** in 11:27–28 as one who hears the word of God and obeys it (see 8:19–21), thus echoing the descriptions of Mary in the infancy narrative. The sign for this generation (11:29–32) is Jonah's preaching of repentance to non-Jews in Nineveh and the Gentile Queen of Sheba seeking out Solomon and his wisdom. These two biblical examples suggest that non-Jews will eventually (especially in Acts, but see also Luke 7:1–10) respond positively to Jesus and his wisdom, and they will seek him out as even greater than Solomon. While this sign may be as clear as a lamp shining in the darkness, those whose spiritual vision is darkened still fail to see and understand it (11:33–36).

The invitation for Jesus to dine at the house of a Pharisee (11:37) provides the occasion for Jesus to issue **a series of "woes"** (see 6:24–26), first against the Pharisees (11:38–44) and then against the lawyers or scribes (11:45–52). He accuses the Pharisees of being more concerned with the externals of piety and their public reputation for holiness than with justice and mercy. He accuses the lawyers of burdening others, living in the past and not the present, and preventing others from gaining true knowledge. Jesus' criticisms result in increased hostility from the scribes and Pharisees (11:53–54).

Having been warned against the hypocrisy of the Pharisees (12:1–3), the followers of Jesus are encouraged to fear God alone and to acknowledge Jesus as the Son of Man before others (12:4–12). The **unforgivable sin** seems to be attributing the work of the Holy Spirit to an evil spirit. The Holy Spirit in turn will remain faithful to those who remain faithful to Jesus and the Spirit.

The place of material goods in the spiritual life is treated in 12:13–34. When asked to adjudicate a family dispute about an inheritance, Jesus instead tells a parable about a rich man whose primary concern was adding to his already abundant wealth, only to find his life cut short by a sudden death. Because he never got to enjoy the results of his labors and had to leave his fortune to others, he is rightly labeled a rich fool. Then in 12:22–34 Jesus issues a series of sayings about trusting in God's providential care for us rather than in material goods and being more concerned with heavenly treasures than with earthly possessions. The implication is that if we truly strive for God's kingdom, God will provide what we really need.

The four master-servant parables in 12:35–48 illustrate the attitude of constant watchfulness or vigilance that followers of Jesus should display in the face of the coming of the Son of Man (for Luke and his readers, Jesus' second coming, or *parousia*). Servants should always be ready for their master's return home (12:35–38). If the home owner knows when the thief is coming, he will be prepared to stop the thief; since the exact time of the Son of Man's arrival remains unknown, one should always be on guard (12:39–40). The manager of the household who is always prepared will be rewarded by the master on his unexpected return, whereas the manager who lives in dissipation during the master's absence will be severely punished on his unexpected return (12:41–46). Servants who know the master's will but disregard it will be punished more severely than those who do not know it, on the grounds that those "to whom much has been given, much will be required" (12:47–48).

The remainder of the first half of the journey narrative (12:49—13:30) consists of various teachings about **the full coming of God's kingdom and gaining admission to it**. With the images of bringing fire and undergoing death by drowning (one meaning of "baptism"), Jesus in 12:49–50 promises a time of testing and cites the extreme case of conflict within the family (12:51–53). In 12:54–56 he calls for discerning the signs of the times in the present and in 12:57–59 for decisive and shrewd action in settling conflicts with opponents. In 13:1–5 Jesus takes two cases of sudden and violent death and uses them as warnings to repent now, while in the parable of the barren fig tree (13:6–9) he evokes the patience and mercy of God. The healing of the crippled woman (13:10–17) illustrates both the compassion of Jesus and his sovereignty over the Sabbath. The twin parables of the mustard seed and the yeast (13:18–21) suggest that from the small beginnings of Jesus' ministry will grow God's kingdom in its fullness. With the parable of the narrow door (13:22–27) Jesus challenges his questioner to respond to his preaching now lest he be denied admission to the banquet that will be part of God's kingdom. Simply belonging to Israel as the people of God is not sufficient. Indeed, according to 13:28–30, some surprising persons will join the great patriarchs, while others (including some Israelites) will be denied admission.

For Reflection and Discussion

What have you learned about discipleship thus far in the journey narrative?

What strikes you most about what Jesus said and did?

5

Jesus' Journey to Jerusalem, Part 2

Luke 13:31—19:27

Luke 13:31–33 makes it clear that **Jesus is going to Jerusalem**, and why.

The occasion is a warning from some Pharisees that Herod Antipas, the ruler in Galilee who had John the Baptist killed, now wants to kill Jesus. Jesus leaves Galilee, however, not to escape from Herod Antipas but rather to go to Jerusalem as the place where prophets die: "it is impossible for a prophet to be killed outside of Jerusalem" (13:33). Even though according to Luke's chronology (based on Mark) Jesus as an adult has not yet visited Jerusalem, he is convinced that he will be rejected and put to death there. His lament over Jerusalem in 13:34–35 reaffirms his identity as a prophet, since in form and content it stands in line with the style and words of the great biblical prophets, Isaiah, Jeremiah, and Ezekiel.

Although in Luke's Gospel the Pharisees are generally hostile to Jesus, in 14:1–24 they once more invite him to dinner (see 7:36–50; 11:37–54). For the Pharisees meals were important occasions for fellowship and sharing wisdom. The fact that **Jesus healed a man with dropsy** (14:1–6) on the Sabbath at a banquet given by a Pharisee would have been controversial and even provocative for both its timing and location. The Pharisees might have agreed that it was lawful to save a life on Sabbath. Their objection to Jesus' action was based on their conviction that he could have waited to perform the healing of this non-life-threatening condition until the Sabbath was over. To them Jesus' behavior was provocative, while for Luke it was a sign of Jesus' sovereignty over the Sabbath.

Jesus' first instruction (14:7–11) concerns **places of honor at a banquet**. As a wise teacher, Jesus recommends taking lowly places on the grounds that if you are told to "move up higher," the other guests will see you and that will increase your honor among them. On the contrary, being asked to leave a seat of honor and go to a lower seat would bring shame. His second instruction (14:12–14) concerns those who might be invited to a banquet. The resurrection of the dead and rewards and punishments after death were characteristic beliefs of the Pharisees. Jesus challenges them to live up to their core beliefs, urging them to invite persons who might be unable to recompense or profit them in this life. They should be satisfied with being rewarded by God at the last judgment.

The introduction to **the parable of the great supper** (14:15–24) signals that its real topic is the kingdom of God. Someone says, "Blessed is anyone who will eat bread in the kingdom of God," and Jesus responds with this parable: A man prepares a great feast and sends a slave to invite the guests. However, those whom he invites give all sorts of (relatively serious) excuses and refuse to come. The host gets angry. So he orders the slave to invite "the poor, the crippled, the blind, and the lame" and anyone else who will come and swears that those who had refused to come will not be allowed in. The parable helps illustrate how the elite members of society have rejected Jesus the prophet and his message and how people in society's margins have accepted him.

After the banquet, Jesus challenges the crowds in 14:25–27 to **place following him above their family ties and to embrace the cross in doing so.** The saying foreshadows Jesus' own death by crucifixion, and it provides the occasion for two parables in 14:28–32 about a man building a tower and a king going out to war, which urge prospective disciples to count the cost of following Jesus. To this challenge he adds the demand that his followers be prepared to give up all their possessions (14:33). In this context the saying about salt in 14:34–35 probably describes as useless those who fail to follow Jesus.

The three parables about the lost sheep, the lost coin, and the lost son in 15:1–32 explain and defend Jesus' special concern for the marginal persons in his society. In 15:1–2 we see that tax collectors and sinners have gathered to listen to Jesus. Tax collectors were suspected of dishonesty (by overcharging) and treason (by cooperating with the Romans and their supporters). Sinners were notorious because of their lifestyle and occupations, which left them unwilling or unable to observe the Jewish law in its fullness. On the other hand, the Pharisees were zealous observers of the law and were dedicated to the spiritual renewal of God's

Then he took the twelve aside and said to them, "See, we are going up to Jerusalem, and everything that is written about the Son of Man by the prophets will be accomplished. For he will be handed over to the Gentiles; and he will be mocked and insulted and spat upon. After they have flogged him, they will kill him, and on the third day he will rise again." But they understood nothing about all these things; in fact, what he said was hidden from them, and they did not grasp what was said.

—Luke 18:31–34

holy people, while the scribes were experts in interpreting and applying the law. The latter two groups complain that Jesus welcomes sinners and eats with them. Jesus answers their objection with two short parables and one long parable.

The short parables are twins, with one featuring a shepherd and the other a woman, and they follow the same dynamic. In 15:3–7 the shepherd leaves his ninety-nine sheep to search for his one lost sheep. When he finds it, he rejoices and invites his friends to share his joy. Likewise in 15:8–10 the woman who loses one of her ten coins does whatever she can to find it. When she does find the coin, she rejoices and invites her friends to share her joy. Both parables end with an application, reminding the Pharisees and scribes that there is great joy in heaven over the repentance of those who may seem to be lost. Both parables suggest that God— and by extension, Jesus—actively seeks those who are lost.

Usually referred to as **the parable of the prodigal son** (15:11–32), the parable of the lost son really has the father as its central character. The father goes out to meet the lost son, forgives him, and restores him to the household. If the lost son was prodigal in the negative sense of squandering his inheritance, the father is prodigal in the positive sense of showing mercy to his son and celebrating his return in a lavish way. The elder son represents people like the Pharisees and scribes who fail to recognize the moral miracle taking place before their eyes with the repentance of tax collectors and sinners through the ministry of Jesus. We are not told whether the elder son accepted his father's explanation ("we had to celebrate") and entered into the festivities.

Most of Luke 16 deals with **money matters**. The parable of the dishonest manager (16:1–8) concerns a rich man who learns that his steward has been squandering his money and demands an accounting before dismissing him. Faced with few other prospects, the manager devises a scheme by which he writes off some of the debts owed to his master. Whether he was involving others in his dishonesty or merely forgoing his own commission, is not clear. What is clear (and surprising) is that the employer praises his shrewdness, and Jesus cites it as an example of how the people of this world are more clever than the children of light. Attached to this parable are sayings about the proper use of earthly goods: use wealth to make friends who can help you (16:9), act honestly and faithfully in financial matters (16:10–12), and recognize that no one can serve two masters, in this case God and money (16:13).

After criticizing the Pharisees as "lovers of money," Luke presents three sayings on various topics. The first saying (16:15) contrasts those who justify themselves (as the Pharisees do) and the true judgment that only God can give. The second saying (16:16–17) makes a division in salvation history between the time of the law and the prophets (up to John the Baptist) and the special time in which Jesus proclaims God's kingdom. The third saying (16:18) seems to be an absolute prohibition of divorce and remarriage.

The topic of money returns in **the parable of the rich man and Lazarus** (16:19–31). During their lifetimes the two characters lived very differently. The rich man wore expensive clothes and feasted every day, while the poor man barely survived by begging. When they die, however, their fates are reversed. The poor man finds rest in Abraham's bosom (something like heaven), while the rich man goes to Hades (something like hell). When the rich man tries to persuade Abraham to show him mercy, he is told that there is a "great chasm" between the two places. When he tries to convince Abraham to send a messenger to his five brothers, he is told that they already have Moses and the prophets to warn them about sharing their material goods. The message of the parable is to share what you have now, before it is too late.

Between the parable of the rich man and Lazarus and the account about the healing of the ten lepers, Luke in 17:1–10 inserts **Jesus' teachings on various aspects of discipleship.** He first warns his followers to avoid being the occasion of another's sin (17:1–2) and then advises that sinners who repent should be forgiven even repeatedly (17:3–4). When the apostles ask that Jesus increase their faith, Jesus uses the image of the tiny mustard seed that grows into a great bush to illustrate that even a little faith can have dramatic results (17:5–6). With yet another master-servant parable in 17:7–10, Jesus reminds them that in serving God they are only doing what they ought to do and have no reason to place themselves on the same level as their master.

After another reminder that Jerusalem is the goal of Jesus' journey, Luke in 17:11–19 places **the healing of the ten lepers.** When they call on Jesus for mercy and healing, he tells them to show themselves to the priests, who can confirm that they truly have been healed. But nothing happens to them until they start on their way. Because they act solely on faith in Jesus' command, they are healed on the way. Even more remarkable is that the only healed leper who returns to praise God and to thank Jesus is a Samaritan, a person whose Judaism is questioned by Galileans and Judeans.

The coming of the kingdom of God is the subject from Jesus' discourse in 17:20–37 (see also 12:35–59 and 21:5–38). When asked by some Pharisees when God's kingdom is coming, Jesus insists that "the kingdom of God is among you" (17:21). Indeed, by his wise teaching and miraculous healings, Jesus has already made God's kingdom a present reality. Then addressing his disciples in 17:22–37, he warns against excessive speculations regarding the signs that will precede the full coming of the kingdom. After prophesying once more about his own suffering and rejection (17:25), Jesus uses several short parables about the days of Noah and Lot and about two men in a bed and two women grinding meal in order to emphasize that the Son of Man's coming will be sudden and clear to all: "Where the corpse is, there the vultures will gather" (17:37). There will be no turning back, and his coming will be decisive.

The second block of Jesus' teaching on prayer appears in 18:1–14 (see 11:1–13). To encourage boldness and persistence in prayer, Jesus in 18:1–8 tells the parable of a widow who wears down an unjust judge and finally gets vindication in her legal case. If an unjust judge will yield to the persistence of a defenseless widow (someone with little or no influence or social standing), how much more will God grant our petitions provided that we are bold and persistent. Then to encourage proper respect and humility in prayer, Jesus in 18:9–14 contrasts a Pharisee and a tax collector at prayer. In the Jewish society of Jesus' time the

Pharisee would have been widely admired for his piety, while the tax collector would have been suspected of dishonesty and treason. Nevertheless, the Pharisee's prayer is really a list of his own spiritual accomplishments and is thus an exercise in self-congratulation. But the tax collector's prayer ("God, be merciful to me, a sinner!") is a genuine expression of humility and dependence on God.

From 18:15 to 18:43, Luke uses material from Mark 10:13–52. Despite his disciples' objections, in 18:15–17 **Jesus blesses the little children** and points to them as exemplifying the attitudes necessary for entering God's kingdom—that is, receiving it as a gift and acknowledging dependence on God. In his **conversation with the rich ruler** (18:18–23), Jesus challenges him to give away his possessions and to live in total dependence on God as one of his disciples. In his commentary on the incident (18:24–30) Jesus notes that while it is difficult for the rich to enter God's kingdom, those who follow him in material poverty will enjoy many benefits both in the present and in the age to come. In 18:31–34 Jesus once more prophesies that in Jerusalem he will die and be raised, and once more the disciples fail to understand him (see 9:22, 44–45). Finally in 18:35–43 an unnamed blind man (called Bartimaeus in Mark) begs Jesus as the Son of David to heal him, and on receiving his sight he follows Jesus on the way to Jerusalem.

Jesus' encounter with Zacchaeus in 19:1–10 illustrates once again that suspect social status or occupation does not exclude a person from entering God's kingdom or following Jesus. The episode takes place in Jericho where Zacchaeus is a rich tax collector.

As a result of his encounter with Jesus, Zacchaeus resolves to be an honest and charitable person. **The parable of the "pounds"** in 19:11–27 emphasizes that vigilance in the face of the coming kingdom is not inactivity or passivity. Rather, one must take bold and positive action to enter God's kingdom.

For Reflection and Discussion

What have you learned about the kingdom of God in this second part of the Lucan journey narrative?

Which of Jesus' encounters with other people have impressed you, and why?

6

Jesus' Ministry in Jerusalem
Luke 19:28—21:38

With the infancy narrative Luke's readers have been well prepared for the importance of Jerusalem in the story of Jesus and the Jerusalem temple as the house of Jesus' heavenly Father (2:49). While Luke's account of Jesus' ministry in Jerusalem follows Mark 11:1—13:37 closely, it gives the impression of a much longer period than the few days allowed in Mark's Holy Week chronology.

The long journey narrative reaches its goal in 19:28–40 when Jesus and his companions come to Bethphage and Bethany, two villages east of Jerusalem, and then to the Mount of Olives, on the eastern slope of Jerusalem. There Jesus arranges for what turns into a prophetic demonstration in which **he enters the city on a colt and is heralded as the one "who comes in the name of the Lord"** (Psalm 118:26–27). In modifying the biblical quotation Luke inserts "the king" and provides echoes of the angels' Gloria in 2:14 ("Peace in heaven and glory in the highest heavens"). In Luke's telling, Jesus ignores the Pharisees'

Then he entered the temple and began to drive out those who were selling things there; and he said, "It is written,
   'My house shall be a house of prayer';
   but you have made it a den of robbers."
Every day he was teaching in the temple. The chief priests, the scribes, and the leaders of the people kept looking for a way to kill him; but they did not find anything they could do, for all the people were spellbound by what they heard.

—Luke 19:45–48

request that the demonstration be stopped. In Luke's perspective Jesus the king is taking possession of what is really his own city. However, Jesus' lament over Jerusalem in 19:41–44 reminds readers that Jerusalem will reject Jesus as their king and so will suffer the destruction of the city and its temple (in AD 70) "because you did not recognize the time of your visitation from God" (19:44).

The demonstration continues in 19:45–46 when **Jesus enters the temple area and drives out "those who were selling things there."** His rationale is a combination of Isaiah 56:7 ("My house shall be a house of prayer") and Jeremiah 7:11 ("but you have made it a den of robbers"). According to 19:47–48, Jesus engaged in a fairly lengthy teaching ministry in Jerusalem ("every day he was teaching in the temple"). The hostility of the Jewish leaders toward Jesus and the growing popular interest in him prepare for the series of conflicts or controversies in 20:1–44 in which Jesus at every point shows himself to be wiser than his questioners. While he cleverly escapes their traps, he also increases their hostility toward himself.

The first question (20:1–8) comes from the chief priests, elders, and scribes—the various groups who will instigate the Roman political officials to put Jesus to death. They want to know **the source of Jesus' authority**. But they really are setting a trap for Jesus. Instead of answering directly, Jesus asks them a question about the source of John the Baptist's authority: Was it from God, or was it merely of human origin? Since the leaders foresee losing face with the common people no matter how they answer, they refuse to give Jesus any answer. Thus Jesus eludes their trap.

The parable of the wicked tenants (20:9–19) interrupts the series of debates. While on the surface the parable seems to be only about wicked tenants, it is at its more profound level about the history of salvation. The vineyard is Israel as the people of God; the tenants are the current Jewish leaders; the owner is God; the slaves are the prophets; and the son is Jesus. When the tenants kill the son, the owner comes and gives the vineyard to other leaders. Note that the vineyard is not destroyed. Rather, it is put under new leadership. The new leader is Jesus, the stone whom the builders rejected (see Psalm 118:22). The leaders recognize the point of Jesus' parable, and only their fear of the people prevents them from killing Jesus then and there.

The second question (20:20–26) concerns **whether it is lawful for Jews to pay taxes to the Roman emperor**. Again it is a trap set by the scribes and chief priests. If Jesus says yes, he will offend the nationalist insurgents. If he says no, he will offend the supporters of, and collaborators with, the Herod family and the Roman officials. But Jesus eludes their trap by showing that Jews are already part of the Roman emperor's economic system (since they use Roman coins) and by urging them to take their obligations to God as seriously as they take their obligations to the emperor.

The third question (20:27–40) concerns **the resurrection of the dead**. Here the questioners are Sadducees, the Jewish group that denied the concept of resurrection and rewards and punishments after death. They know that in this matter Jesus sided with the Pharisees. Their example of a woman who married seven brothers in a row, while based on biblical law (see Deuteronomy

25:5), is designed to reduce to absurdity his support for resurrection. However, Jesus eludes their trap by showing that they do not understand resurrection (there will be no marriage then) or the Scriptures (according to Exodus 3, the great patriarchs are still alive).

The fourth question (20:41–44) concerns **the proper title for the Son of David or Messiah.** According to Psalm 110:1, David says that the Lord (God) called the new king and descendant of David "my Lord." The implication is that Jesus is superior (as "my Lord") to David himself and that "Lord" is an even greater and more appropriate title for him than "Son of David" or "Messiah."

The debates are rounded off by a **comparison between the scribes (20:45–47) who pretend to be religious but are really hypocritical predators, and a poor widow (21:1–4) who contributes all she has to the temple treasury.**

Luke places Jesus' final (or eschatological) discourse (21:5–38) in the context of his daily ministry at the Jerusalem temple (see 21:5, 37–38). While taking much of his material from Mark 13, Luke rearranges it to lengthen the timetable of events. The occasion for the discourse is **Jesus' prophecy of the temple's destruction** ("not one stone will be left"). When the disciples ask about when this will happen and what signs will accompany it, Jesus warns against being led astray by deceivers. There will be signs such as wars, earthquakes, famines, plagues, and cosmic portents. But "before all this occurs" (21:12) there will be persecutions, divisions within families, and hatred. However, the followers of Jesus should remember that all these events will lead to the fullness of God's kingdom and their redemption: "By your endurance you will gain your souls" (21:19).

In a passage unique to this Gospel (21:20–24), **Jesus describes the destruction of Jerusalem** in such a way as to suggest that the wording has been influenced by what actually took place in AD 70 when the Romans destroyed Jerusalem. Only after the "times of the Gentiles are fulfilled" will the cosmic portents and the coming of the Son of Man occur (21:25–28). When the proper time arrives, it will be obvious to all (21:29–33). As in 21:19, all these events are part of the full coming of God's kingdom and so involve the vindication and redemption of the wise and righteous followers of Jesus. The proper attitude in the present (21:34–36) is constant vigilance and prayer for strength in the trials to come (see 11:4). Luke concludes in 21:37–38 that Jesus' daily instructions in the temple area drew large and enthusiastic responses from the common people, despite the growing hostility of their leaders.

For Reflection and Discussion

What does Jesus mean when he says "the kingdom of God is among you" (17:21)?

Why do Jesus' words and actions cause so much conflict? Can you imagine any way he could have avoided such conflict?

7

Jesus' Passion, Death, and Resurrection in Jerusalem

Luke 22:1—24:53

The account of Jesus' passion, death, and resurrection in Jerusalem serves as the climax of Luke's narrative about Jesus. His primary source was Mark 14—16, to which he added some independent traditions and his own literary touches. In this way he highlights Jesus as an innocent martyr or witness, who to the end of his life practices his teachings about fidelity to God, concern for the poor, and love of enemies. Thus he continues to proclaim his good news (see Luke 4:18–19) even from the cross. And even after his resurrection and ascension, Jesus can still be encountered through the Old Testament Scriptures and in the community's meals.

The plot to kill Jesus (22:1–6) takes place shortly before Passover, the spring festival celebrating ancient Israel's liberation from slavery in Egypt. Passover was one of the great pilgrimage festivals that attracted large crowds to Jerusalem and its temple (see 2:41–52). The chief priests and scribes are afraid that Jesus'

But on the first day of the week, at early dawn, they came to the tomb, taking the spices that they had prepared. They found the stone rolled away from the tomb, but when they went in, they did not find the body. While they were perplexed about this, suddenly two men in dazzling clothes stood beside them. The women were terrified and bowed their faces to the ground, but the men said to them, "Why do you look for the living among the dead? He is not here, but has risen."

—Luke 24:1–5

presence might spark off a riot or a political uprising. The willingness of Judas Iscariot, one of Jesus' closest followers, to join their plot makes their work easier. While acknowledging that Judas was paid for his participation, Luke tells us first that "Satan entered into Judas." Since the last temptation of Jesus (4:13), Satan has been off the stage. Now Luke suggests that in the Passion narrative Satan's activity is going to be a major force in the events leading up to Jesus' death.

Luke follows Mark in interpreting Jesus' last supper as an official Passover meal (whereas John places it before the Passover festival begins). In caring for the **preparation of the meal** (22:7–13) Jesus takes the initiative and gives the impression of having made all the arrangements before sending Peter and John to carry them out. Right from the start of the Passion narrative, the reader gets the impression that Jesus is in command of the events that are about to unfold.

The scene for **Jesus' last supper** (22:14–23) is a large upper room in Jerusalem, and there Jesus takes his place at the table along with his apostles. While the words that Jesus speaks in Luke's Last Supper account are familiar, their sequence is not. He first announces that this will be his last Passover with them, and he symbolizes this assertion by passing around a cup of wine and declaring that he will not drink wine again "until the kingdom of God comes." Next he takes a loaf of bread, gives thanks, breaks it, passes it around to the apostles, and states, "This is my body, which is given for you. Do this in remembrance of me." Then after supper, he hands around another cup of wine and says, "This cup that is poured out for you is the new covenant in my blood."

Luke's version of the words of institution seem to combine elements from the formulas in Mark 14:22–25 and 1 Corinthians 11:23–26, though their order is unique (the usual order is bread, cup, kingdom saying). At any rate, the many essential theological aspects of the Eucharist are present in Luke's version: Passover context; anticipation of the heavenly banquet in God's kingdom; the identification of the bread and wine with Jesus' body and blood; Jesus' death as a sacrifice; the supper as a memorial; and the new covenant.

As a sequel to the Last Supper, Luke provides Jesus with a **farewell discourse** (or testament) in 22:21–38. In 22:21–23, Jesus prophesies that one of those at table will betray him. Even though Jesus' fate as the Son of Man has already been determined through his willingness to do the Father's will, the betrayer (Judas) still bears the responsibility and guilt of the betrayal. Although Jesus seems to know his betrayer's identity, the others do not. This theme of Jesus' foreknowledge indicates that he goes willingly to his fate. When the disciples in 22:24–27 engage in a debate about who is the greatest among them, Jesus affirms that in his community greatness is measured by humble service to others. In this way Jesus prepares the reader to interpret his own suffering and death as humble service to humanity. In 22:28–30 he returns to his theme of the Last Supper being the anticipation of the heavenly banquet in the kingdom of God. In 22:31–34 he issues a prophecy of Peter's threefold denial of Jesus. Finally in 22:35 he urges his disciples to recall how in the past God has cared for them. Now during the Passion, however, in what seems to be a case of gallows humor, Jesus in 22:36–38 says that since he is soon to be counted "among the lawless" (referring to Isaiah 53:12), he and they might as well look the part and so he says that two swords will be enough.

After his Last Supper, **Jesus and his disciples go to the Mount of Olives**, on the eastern slope of Jerusalem (22:39–46). Though he urges his disciples to pray, they quickly fall asleep. By contrast Jesus appears as the obedient martyr who prays at this decisive moment in his life and tries to conform himself to what seems to be the will of his heavenly Father. The "anguish" (from the Greek word *agonia)* that he experiences evokes the image of an athlete immersed in a competition (22:44). The text says that Jesus' sweat came down like drops of blood, not necessarily that he sweated blood.

The arrest of Jesus (22:47–53) is facilitated by Judas leading a crowd and identifying Jesus with a kiss, ironically a sign of respect that a disciple might bestow on his esteemed teacher. Peter's cutting off the ear of the high priest's servant fulfills Jesus' prophecy in 22:36–38. But Jesus immediately forbids any violent defense of himself and heals the man. Then he denies that he is a "bandit" (a term carrying social and political overtones, as "insurgent" does today). His labeling these events as "your hour, and the power of darkness" suggests that his opponents are instruments of Satan (see 22:3).

After his arrest Jesus is taken to the high priest's house, and Peter follows at a safe distance. In 22:54–62 **Peter three times denies knowing Jesus and being one of his disciples**, thus fulfilling Jesus' prophecy in 22:31–34. Only Luke says that "the Lord turned and looked at Peter," thus explaining graphically why Peter then wept bitterly. The soldiers' physical abuse and mockery of Jesus in 22:63–65 and their challenge to him to prophesy reinforce the identification of Jesus as a prophet that Luke has developed throughout the Gospel narrative. His point is that Jesus the prophet cannot be properly understood apart from his passion and death.

In 22:66—23:12 Jesus undergoes a series of trials that help to corroborate his innocence and clarify his identity. In **the trial before the Jewish council** (22:66–71) what is at issue is Jesus' identity as the Messiah, the Son of Man, and the Son of God, all titles bestowed on Jesus throughout Luke's Gospel. Jesus' response, "You say that I am," indicates that it depends on how and by whom these titles are being interpreted. To the Jewish council members, applying these titles to Jesus is blasphemy. The reader of the Gospel, however, is already familiar with them and should by now be convinced that they rightly apply to Jesus.

In **handing Jesus over to the Roman prefect Pontius Pilate** in 23:1–5, the leaders of the Jewish council make three charges against Jesus. They claim that Jesus was perverting the people, forbidding them to pay taxes to the Romans, and claiming to be the Messiah. The third charge gets the most attention from Pilate, who regards Jesus as just another in a series of Jewish political-religious insurgents. Nevertheless, even Pilate concludes that Jesus is really innocent of these charges.

Rather than freeing Jesus, however, in 23:6–12 **Pilate hands him over to Herod Antipas,** the ruler in Galilee, on the grounds that Jesus is a Galilean. While Herod is initially curious about Jesus, the prisoner refuses to cooperate in the proceedings. The chief priests and scribes remain adamant in their accusations against Jesus. After another mockery of Jesus, Herod sends him back to Pilate.

At what turns into **the sentencing of Jesus** (23:13–25), Pilate first publicly declares that Jesus is innocent of the charges against him and plans to have him flogged and released. However, at the instigation of the Jewish leaders, the crowd repeatedly calls for Jesus to be crucified. When given a **choice between Jesus and Barabbas** (an insurgent and a murderer), they prefer that Barabbas be released. And so Pilate gives in, and hands Jesus over to them. Thus Luke places the initiative for Jesus' death on the Jewish officials.

The death sentence is carried out immediately (23:26–31). They enlist Simon of Cyrene to carry the horizontal beam of the cross. As a crowd gathers, Jesus warns the women about even greater sufferings in store for the inhabitants of Jerusalem, thus pointing forward to the city's destruction under the Romans in AD 70.

The crucifixion (23:32–43) takes place at the "Skull"—Calvary—outside Jerusalem. Along with two insurgents, Jesus is crucified as "King of the Jews," the Gentile translation of "Messiah." What was intended as mockery is in fact the truth. Jesus resists all temptations to save himself ("if you are the Son of God," see 4:1–13) and asks his Father to forgive his tormentors and promises the "good thief" a place in paradise with him. Even on the cross Jesus remains committed to the love of enemies and outreach to the marginalized.

In Luke's account, **Jesus' death** (23:44–49) is accompanied by cosmic events and the tearing of the temple curtain. Jesus' last words are a prayer to his heavenly Father. Using the language of Psalm 31, Jesus expresses his trust in and submission to his Father ("into your hands I commend my spirit"). The centurion overseeing the execution affirms Jesus' innocence. While the crowds return home with guilt pangs, the women followers from Galilee (8:1–3) remain at the scene and so can bear witness that Jesus is really dead.

Joseph of Arimathea ("a good and righteous man") sees to **the burial of Jesus** (23:50–56). Luke insists that Joseph did not participate in the Jewish council's condemnation of Jesus. As someone "waiting expectantly for the kingdom of God," Joseph offers to place Jesus' corpse in his burial cave outside the city walls and to see to his entombment before the beginning of the Sabbath at sundown (Friday evening). The same women who saw Jesus die, also see where he is buried.

On Sunday morning these women come to the tomb to tend to Jesus' corpse (24:1–12). But they find the stone that covered the entrance rolled away and the tomb empty. They are told by "two men in dazzling clothes" that Jesus has been raised from the dead just as he himself had prophesied. The women's report to the apostles about the empty tomb is confirmed by Peter when he goes to the tomb and sees for himself that it is empty.

In **the appearance to the two disciples on the road to Emmaus** (24:13–35) the mysterious stranger who turns out to be the risen Jesus explains that the events surrounding his passion and death have occurred in accord with God's will revealed in the Scriptures. The two disciples come to recognize the mysterious stranger as the risen Jesus when they share a meal with him.

The sequence of recognizing the risen Jesus in the Scriptures and the meal is reversed in **the appearance to the disciples gathered in Jerusalem** (24:36–49). As they are sharing a meal, Jesus comes in their midst and emphasizes the physical character of his body by eating some fish. He goes on to explain from the Scriptures that the Messiah had to suffer and rise from the dead. He then commissions his followers to proclaim repentance and forgiveness of sin, "beginning from Jerusalem" (see Acts 1—7).

The ascension of Jesus (24:50–53; see Acts 1:6–11) takes place at Bethany (see 19:29). This event concludes the time of Jesus (the center of time) and sets the stage for the time of the Holy Spirit and the church, which will be described in the Acts of the Apostles.

For Reflection and Discussion

How does Jesus continue his ministry even in the midst of his arrest, trial, and execution?

When you consider the stories in Luke 24 about the resurrected Jesus appearing to the disciples, what do they communicate about the Eucharist we now celebrate in our worship?

PART THREE

Luke's Literary
Artistry

8

Luke as an Interpreter of Traditions

In the preface to his Gospel, Luke claimed to have access to previous accounts of Jesus' sayings and deeds and to have incorporated them into his own "orderly account." Modern scholars have identified at least a few of these sources: the Gospel of Mark, the Sayings Source Q, and some traditions that are unique to Luke's Gospel, referred to as L. Whether L was one source or several is not clear.

The task of discerning the sources used by the Evangelist is called *source criticism*. How Luke modified and adapted his sources is called *redaction* (or editorial) *criticism*. This kind of analysis can help us become more sensitive to Luke's distinctive theological emphases. Luke's use of sources represents his interpretation of the early Christian tradition and provides guidance for our own personal and pastoral use of his Gospel today.

A. Luke's Use of Various Sources

Luke's account of the ministry of John the Baptist at the beginning of his narrative about Jesus' career as an adult in 3:1–20 can give us an initial snapshot of Luke's practices and skills as an editor and interpreter. By analyzing this material we can see firsthand that Luke is both a faithful transmitter of tradition and a creative interpreter of it.

The Preaching of John the Baptist

Mark began his Gospel "in the middle of things," with John the Baptist and Jesus as adults. There is no infancy narrative in Mark.

Mark 1:1–6

The beginning of the good news of Jesus Christ, the Son of God. As it is written in the prophet Isaiah, "See, I am sending my messenger ahead of you,
  who will prepare your way;
the voice of one crying out in the wilderness:
  'Prepare the way of the Lord,
  make his paths straight,' "

John the baptizer appeared in the wilderness, proclaiming a baptism of repentance for the forgiveness of sins. And people from the whole Judean countryside and all the people of Jerusalem were going out to him, and were baptized by him in the river Jordan, confessing their sins. Now John was clothed with camel's hair, with a leather belt around his waist, and he ate locusts and wild honey.

After identifying the topic of his Gospel ("the good news of Jesus Christ, the Son of God") Mark combines and attributes to Isaiah prophecies from Exodus 23:20 and Malachi 3:1 ("See, I am sending my messenger") and Isaiah 40:3 ("the voice of one crying out in the wilderness"). Then he describes John's preaching ("a baptism of repentance for the forgiveness of sins"), the popular response that John received, and his lifestyle, which evokes that of the prophet Elijah (see 2 Kings 1:8). What does Luke do with this material?

Luke 3:1–6

In the fifteenth year of the reign of Emperor Tiberius, when Pontius Pilate was governor of Judea, and Herod was ruler of Galilee, and his brother Philip ruler of the region of Ituraea and Trachonitis, and Lysanias ruler of Abilene, during the high priesthood of Annas and Caiaphas, the word of God came to John son of Zechariah in the wilderness. He went into all the region around the Jordan, proclaiming a baptism of repentance for the forgiveness of sins, as it is written in the book of the words of the prophet Isaiah,

"The voice of one crying out in the wilderness:
'Prepare the way of the Lord,
    make his paths straight.
Every valley shall be filled,
    and every mountain and hill shall be made low,
and the crooked shall be made straight,
    and the rough ways made smooth;
and all flesh shall see the salvation of God.'"

Since Luke has already introduced John the Baptist and Jesus at some length in the infancy narrative, there was no need for him to reproduce Mark's title sentence (1:1). Instead Luke places the adult ministries of John and Jesus in the wider context of history by mentioning in 3:1–2 the political and religious leaders active in the Roman Empire and in the land of Israel during the fifteenth year of the emperor Tiberius (AD 28 or 29). All of these figures except Lysanias will reappear in Luke's narrative. This construction gives the impression that this was the right time for the divine plan being fulfilled in John and Jesus to begin unfolding.

In describing John, Luke identifies him as a prophet ("the word of God came to John") and summarizes the information about him from Mark 1:4–6. In 1:17 Luke had already identified John with Elijah, and so there was no need here to allude to their common lifestyle. Luke recognized that the first part of the biblical quotation did not come from Isaiah and so he omitted it (only to use it later in 7:27). Instead he has extended the quotation of Isaiah 40:3 to include the next two verses, most likely in order to emphasize from the start that Jesus will bring about God's salvation for "all flesh."

John's Preaching, Part 1

The first sample of John's preaching is generally assigned to the Sayings Source Q. There is no extant ancient manuscript of Q available to us today. Scholars have formed this hypothesis upon the close correspondences in material found in the Gospels of Matthew and Luke but not in Mark. In many cases the wording is so close that one must suspect the use of a common source. This common source Q seems to have been a collection of Jesus' sayings that circulated in early Christian circles before the Gospels of Matthew and Luke were composed. It is supposed that those two Evangelists had access to and used Q independently. In general, Luke is regarded as the more conservative editor of Q, while Matthew tends to be freer in his use of this source.

According to Luke, this first sample of John's preaching was directed to "the crowds that came out to be baptized by him," whereas according to Matthew it was aimed at "many Pharisees and Sadducees coming for baptism." The Q version most likely did not specify the audience at all, and each Evangelist tailored the speech to a specific audience that especially concerned him. In Matthew's Gospel the Pharisees and Sadducees often appear as opponents of Jesus, while Luke tends to emphasize the wider, universal significance of both John and Jesus and so in his account the "crowds" are the main audience.

The wording of John's discourse in Luke and Matthew is almost exactly the same in both the NRSV translation and in the original Greek text. Either one Evangelist was copying from the other, or (what is more likely) both used a common written source.

Here is John's speech according to Luke:

Luke 3:7–9
John said to the crowds that came out to be baptized by him, "You brood of vipers! Who warned you to flee from the wrath to come? Bear fruits worthy of repentance. Do not begin to say to yourselves,

'We have Abraham as our ancestor'; for I tell you, God is able from these stones to raise up children to Abraham. Even now the axe is lying at the root of the trees; every tree therefore that does not bear good fruit is cut down and thrown into the fire."

And here is John's speech according to Matthew:

Matthew 3:7–10.
But when he saw many Pharisees and Sadducees coming for baptism, he said to them, "You brood of vipers! Who warned you to flee from the wrath to come? Bear fruit worthy of repentance. Do not presume to say to yourselves, 'We have Abraham as our ancestor'; for I tell you, God is able from these stones to raise up children to Abraham. Even now the axe is lying at the root of the trees; every tree therefore that does not bear good fruit is cut down and thrown into the fire."

The horizon for John's discourse is "the wrath to come," the judgment that will accompany the full coming of God's kingdom. John first warns that accepting his baptism also demands sincere repentance and doing good deeds. Next he warns that merely belonging to the children of Abraham (and Israel as God's chosen people) is not enough to protect a person in the coming judgment. Then he warns that since the time is short, people should be careful to bear good fruit in what time remains. So in this case both Luke and Matthew seem to have preserved the text much as they found it in Q, and both assigned it an audience in keeping with their own audiences and concerns.

John's Preaching, Part 2

The second sample of John's preaching appears only in Luke's Gospel and so is assigned the label "L," meaning that it contains special Lucan material.

> Luke 3:10–14
> And the crowds asked him, "What then should we do?" In reply he said to them, "Whoever has two coats must share with anyone who has none; and whoever has food must do likewise." Even tax collectors came to be baptized, and they asked him, "Teacher, what should we do?" He said to them, "Collect no more than the amount prescribed for you." Soldiers also asked him, "And we, what should we do?" He said to them, "Do not extort money from anyone by threats or false accusation, and be satisfied with your wages."

In this passage Luke provides positive advice to three groups of people, thus balancing the negative warnings in 3:7–9.

It's not clear whether Luke took 3:10–14 from a source or composed it on his own. In either case, he introduces some characters—crowds, tax collectors, and soldiers—who appear later in his narrative. Moreover, the themes introduced here by John the Baptist—willingness to share with others now, honesty to be practiced by tax collectors, and positive relations with soldiers—occur also in the body of the Gospel (see Luke 7:1–10; 16:19–31; 19:1–10) and in Acts.

John's Preaching, Part 3

In the third sample of John's preaching, Luke constructs a narrative framework at the beginning and end, and in between he places a contrast between John's baptism and Jesus' baptism that is found apparently in both Mark and Q, and then repeats a warning from Q about the nearness of the coming judgment.

Luke 3:15–18

As the people were filled with expectation, and all were questioning in their hearts concerning John, whether he might be the Messiah, John answered all of them by saying, "I baptize you with water; but one who is more powerful than I is coming; I am not worthy to untie the thong of his sandals. He will baptize you with the Holy Spirit and fire. His winnowing fork is in his hand, to clear his threshing floor and to gather the wheat into his granary; but the chaff he will burn with unquenchable fire." So, with many other exhortations, he proclaimed the good news to the people.

The introduction in 3:15 with its double mention of "all" heightens expectations for what follows. The conclusion in 3:18 brings together all the parts of John's preaching and other speeches not found in this Gospel under the heading of "good news to the people."

The traditional saying in Luke 3:16 (compare Mark 1:7–8; Matthew 3:11) emphasizes that Jesus as a person is mightier than John (just as a master is mightier than his slave) and that Jesus' baptism in the "Holy Spirit and fire" is more powerful than John's baptism in water only. There may well have been some overlap here between Mark and Q on the wording of this saying, which would explain the agreement in "with the Holy Spirit and fire" between Matthew and Luke against Mark. The warning in 3:17 is clearly from Q. It uses traditional Jewish imagery for the last judgment and indicates that the judgment separating good and evil persons is near.

John's Imprisonment

In Mark 6:17–29 (and Matthew 14:3–12), the story of John's arrest and imprisonment under Herod Antipas is told at length in a kind of flashback. Here Luke has taken material from Mark, summarized it, and placed it before Jesus begins his public ministry.

> Luke 3:19–20
>
> But Herod the ruler, who had been rebuked by him because of Herodias, his brother's wife, and because

of all the evil things that Herod had done, added to
them all by shutting up John in prison.

The effect of this placement is to get John off the stage before
Jesus begins his public activity. It does, however, raise the question:
Who baptized Jesus? Luke's editorial move seems to reflect
his three-stage organization of salvation history. John belonged
to the period of Israel and the Old Testament, while Jesus' public
preaching inaugurates a new era in which all the energies of the
Holy Spirit are focused on him. See Luke 16:16: "The law and
the prophets were in effect until John came; since then the good
news of the kingdom of God is proclaimed."

With his inclusion of material from various sources and his
careful editing of them, Luke places the story of John and Jesus
in the context of world history, shows John to be subordinate to
Jesus (who brings the salvation of God), instructs all kinds of
people to prepare negatively and positively for the coming judgment,
highlights the superiority of Jesus' person and baptism,
and signals the new phase of salvation history to be inaugurated
with Jesus' appearance on the public stage.

B. Luke and Q: Blessings and Woes

The first large block of Jesus' teachings in Luke's Gospel is
called the Sermon on the Plain (6:20–49). In Luke's theological
geography the plain, or level place, is where Jesus meets the
crowds and teaches them there. A different theological geography
is reflected in what is commonly known as the Sermon on

the Mount in Matthew 5—7. There the mountain is the place of divine revelation.

Both Matthew and Luke seem to have used independently the Sayings Source Q to develop their versions of Jesus' inaugural sermon. It is generally agreed that Luke's version is closer to what they found in Q and that Matthew has expanded greatly the Q sermon and used it as a vehicle for including many teachings attributed to Jesus in other traditions.

Both Evangelists preface their versions of Jesus' discourse with a series of blessings, or beatitudes. While in Matthew's version there are nine beatitudes, in Luke's version there are only four:

Luke 6:20–23
Then he looked up at his disciples and said:
"Blessed are you who are poor,
     for yours is the kingdom of God.
"Blessed are you who are hungry now,
     for you will be filled.
"Blessed are you who weep now,
     for you will laugh.
"Blessed are you when people hate you, and when
they exclude you, revile you, and defame you on
account of the Son of Man. Rejoice in that day and
leap for joy, for surely your reward is great in heaven;
for that is what their ancestors did to the prophets.

A beatitude declares someone to be happy, fortunate, or lucky. This literary form is common in the Old Testament wisdom writings and Psalms. Indeed, the book of Psalms begins with a beatitude: "Happy are those who do not follow the advice of the wicked" (1:1). A person may be declared happy or blessed because of some virtue, attitude, or possession. In the Dead Sea Scrolls and other early Jewish writings there is a tendency to bring together a wisdom element and the promise of a future reward when God's kingdom comes in its fullness. So we can suppose that when Luke introduced his first substantial sample of Jesus' teachings, he had access to the short sermon in Q that began with a series of beatitudes containing both a wisdom element and an eschatological promise.

The beatitudes in Luke's Gospel are expressed in the second person plural form ("you who are poor"). The four beatitudes in Luke 6:20–23 declare "blessed" or "happy" those who are poor, hungry, weeping, and hated or persecuted. These are not the kinds of people declared to be blessed in the Old Testament or other early Jewish writings. The second part of each Lucan beatitude contains the promise of a radical change and a corresponding reward. The basic reward is the kingdom of God. From this reward the others follow: being filled, laughing, and rejoicing at the prospect of a heavenly reward. The Lucan beatitudes describe the great reversal that will come about with the fullness of God's kingdom. They echo the reversal theme at the heart of Mary's song in Luke 1:46–55: "He has brought down the powerful from their thrones, and lifted up the lowly."

We can grasp the distinctive character of the Lucan beatitudes by comparing them with Matthew 5:3–12. In Matthew's version, the beatitudes are presented in the third person plural form ("Blessed are the poor in spirit, for theirs is the kingdom of heaven"). This is by far the more customary form of beatitudes in the Old Testament and early Jewish writings. Moreover, Matthew includes nine beatitudes rather than four. Whether Matthew composed them by himself or appropriated them from another tradition is not clear. The four beatitudes from the Q sermon (poor, weeping, hungry, persecuted) provided the foundation, while the additional beatitudes filled out the picture of what virtues, values, and attitudes should characterize the followers of Jesus. Also there is a tendency on Matthew's part to spiritualize (and therefore make more universal) several of the Q beatitudes: poor *in spirit*, hungering and thirsting *for righteousness*, and persecuted *for the sake of righteousness*.

While Matthew expands the Q beatitudes by adding five more to the list, Luke does something similar by adding four "woes":

> Luke 6:24–26
> "But woe to you who are rich,
>   for you have received your consolation.
> "Woe to you who are full now,
>   for you will be hungry.
> "Woe to you who are laughing now,
>   for you will mourn and weep.
> "Woe to you when all speak well of you, for that is
> what their ancestors did to the false prophets.

A woe is the negative equivalent of a beatitude. It warns that severe punishment will come as the result of certain vices or bad behaviors. It was used especially by the biblical prophets.

The four Lucan woes are the mirror image of the four Q beatitudes. They keep the second person plural format. They warn the rich, the full, the laughing, and the famous that they have already experienced their share of happiness and that in the great reversal they will become poor, hungry, weeping, and hated. The great reversal is the full coming of God's kingdom. Luke's addition of the four woes was his way of underscoring the change that will come about then.

What do the blessings and the woes in Luke tell us about Luke as a transmitter of traditions? In the part devoted to the beatitudes Luke appears to have been a faithful transmitter of what he found in the Sayings Source Q. He retains the second person plural format ("Blessed are you who are") and the concrete content (poor, hungry, weeping, hated) that seem to have been present in Q. By contrast Matthew adjusted the form to fit the more usual Jewish pattern ("Blessed are they"), expanded the content in a more spiritual direction ("Blessed are the poor in spirit"), and added five more beatitudes. In this instance Luke proves to be the more conservative editor of Q (as he usually is). Nevertheless, by adding the four woes that mirror the four beatitudes, Luke puts his own stamp on the Q material included in his Sermon on the Plain.

C. Luke and Mark: The Agony in the Garden

Between the Last Supper and the arrest of Jesus, the Gospel Passion narratives include the scene of Jesus at prayer in Gethsemane, a small olive garden outside the city wall of Jerusalem, on its eastern slope. In this episode Jesus the obedient Son of God accepts the fate of suffering and death before him as being in accord with God's will.

Mark contains a lengthy and detailed account of the episode:

Mark 14:32–42

They went to a place called Gethsemane; and he said to his disciples, "Sit here while I pray." He took with him Peter and James and John, and began to be distressed and agitated. And he said to them, "I am deeply grieved, even to death; remain here, and keep awake." And going a little farther, he threw himself on the ground and prayed that, if it were possible, the hour might pass from him. He said, "Abba, Father, for you all things are possible; remove this cup from me; yet, not what I want, but what you want." He came and found them sleeping; and he said to Peter, "Simon, are you asleep? Could you not keep awake one hour? Keep awake and pray that you may not come into the time of trial; the spirit indeed is willing, but the flesh is weak." And again he went away and prayed, saying the same words. And once more he came and found them sleeping, for their eyes were very heavy; and they did not know what to say to him. He came a third time and said to them, "Are you still sleeping and taking your rest? Enough! The hour has come; the Son of Man is betrayed into the hands of sinners. Get up, let us be going. See, my betrayer is at hand."

Mark sets the scene by providing the name of the place ("Gethsemane") and naming Peter, James, and John again as the inner circle among Jesus' disciples (see Mark 5:37; 9:2). In describing Jesus, Mark emphasizes the deep emotions that the prospect of suffering and death has stirred in Jesus: "[he] began to be distressed and agitated. . . . I am deeply grieved." In 14:35–36 Mark first paraphrases the prayer and then quotes it: "Abba, Father, for you all things are possible; remove this cup from me; yet not what I want, but what you want." Then Jesus comes to the disciples three times, and each time he finds them sleeping despite his initial instruction to them to stay awake. Finally, Jesus announces that "the hour has come" and urges that the events that now seem inevitable should proceed. Mark's account emphasizes that Jesus, after some serious struggle, accepts his passion and death as God's will and contrasts his strength with the disciples, whose spirit may be willing but whose flesh is weak.

Luke shortens, reshapes, and simplifies Mark's account rather radically.

Luke 22:39–46

He came out and went, as was his custom, to the Mount of Olives; and the disciples followed him. When he reached the place, he said to them, "Pray that you may not come into the time of trial." Then he withdrew from them about a stone's throw, knelt down, and prayed, "'Father, if you are willing, remove this cup from me; yet, not my will but yours be done." [Then an angel from heaven appeared to him and gave him strength. In his anguish he prayed more earnestly, and his sweat became like great drops of blood falling down on the ground.] When he got up from prayer, he came to the disciples and found them sleeping because of grief, and he said to them, "Why are you sleeping? Get up and pray that you may not come into the time of trial."

Luke locates the episode on the Mount of Olives and omits the names of the disciples. The instruction to them ("Pray that you may not come into the time of trial") echoes the final petition in the Lord's Prayer ("And do not bring us to the time of trial," 11:4) and places the event in the context of end-time testing. Jesus' prayer addresses God simply as "Father" and includes the provision "if you are willing." (The addition in 22:43–44 will be discussed below.) At the end of the prayer Jesus visits the disciples only once, and Luke explains that they were sleeping "because of grief." Finally, Jesus awakens the disciples in the hope that they may not "come into the time of trial."

The effect of Luke's editing of the Marcan version is to highlight the centrality of Jesus at prayer. Throughout Luke's narrative Jesus prays at the decisive moments in his ministry. The emphasis on Jesus at prayer marks this event as important. As Jesus does regularly, he addresses God as his Father and so calls attention to his unique relationship with God. At this point he proves himself to be in perfect alignment with his Father's will. At the same time Luke softens Mark's harsh image of Jesus' disciples. He attributes their sleeping to "grief," places their sleeping in the context of trials, and relates that Jesus criticizes them not three times but only once.

The most distinctive part of Luke's account of Jesus in Gethsemane may not come from Luke at all. According to 22:43–44, "an angel from heaven appeared and gave him strength. In his anguish he prayed more earnestly, and his sweat became like great drops of blood on the ground." These verses are absent from many of the earliest and best Greek manuscripts of Luke's Gospel, and many textual critics contend that they are later additions to Luke's text. That is why in modern editions of the Greek New Testament and the translations made on the basis of them, it has become customary to place them in brackets. Nevertheless, some early manuscripts do include them, and some early Christian writers refer to them. So it is at least conceivable that Luke wrote these verses or took them from one of his sources.

It is from Luke 22:44 that we get the expression "the agony in the garden." The Greek word *agonia* often describes an athletic competition and fits well with Luke's portrayal of Jesus as a martyr who engages in a contest and remains faithful to God in his struggle. The appearance of the angel in 22:43 recalls the angelic interventions that are prominent in the infancy narrative. The emphasis on Jesus at prayer also fits nicely with Luke's development of that theme throughout his narrative. The sweat "like great drops of blood" further contributes to the theme of Jesus as a martyr in the face of suffering. Whether Luke wrote these verses or a later scribe added them here, they do contribute to several themes that are prominent in Luke's Gospel: angelic interventions, Jesus' death as a martyrdom, and Jesus praying at decisive moments.

What we have seen in these passages from Luke's Gospel can be easily replicated in many other texts. This kind of exercise in source criticism and redaction criticism gives us some sense of the care with which the Evangelist whom we call Luke handed on and interpreted the early traditions about Jesus as he carried out his task of providing his orderly account concerning "the events that have been fulfilled among us" (1:1).

For Reflection and Discussion

Why is it so important to understand Luke's work as an editor—that is, as a transmitter and interpreter of traditions?

What do you especially appreciate about Luke's treatment of Jesus' story—or what do you not appreciate about it, and why?

9

Ten Themes in Luke

The narrative analysis of Luke's Gospel in chapters 2—7 has shown that the Evangelist was an effective storyteller, a master of character development and plot. The examples in chapter 8 of Luke's skill as a faithful transmitter and creative interpreter of traditional sources reinforce the impression that we are in the presence of a skilled literary artist.

Luke communicates his message of the faith in another way, by developing themes that run through his Gospel and into the Acts of the Apostles. We can better appreciate Luke's artistry and theology by paying attention to these themes. As always, for Luke, truth is in the details.

1. Salvation History

Luke seems to see the history of salvation as divided into three great periods: the time of Israel or the Old Testament, the time of Jesus, and the time of the Holy Spirit or the church. The time of Israel includes John the Baptist. That is why Luke recounts

91

Soon afterwards he went on through cities and villages, proclaiming and bringing the good news of the kingdom of God. The twelve were with him, as well as some women who had been cured of evil spirits and infirmities; Mary, called Magdalene, from whom seven demons had gone out, and Joanna, the wife of Herod's steward Chuza, and Susanna, and many others, who provided for them out of their resources.

—Luke 8:1–3

John's arrest and imprisonment before the baptism of Jesus (see Luke 3:19–20) and why Jesus says in 16:16 that "the law and the prophets were in effect until John came." The time of Jesus' public activity constitutes the middle or center of time. It is the great "today" or "now," when all the power of the Holy Spirit is concentrated on the person of Jesus. This period lasts until Jesus' ascension. The story of Jesus is the core event in God's plan of redemptive history. The time of the Holy Spirit or the church begins with the descent of the Holy Spirit upon the first disciples in Jerusalem at Pentecost (see Acts 2). While rooted in Judaism (as the Lucan infancy narrative makes clear), the movement begun by Jesus is open to non-Jews (see Luke 4:16–30) and poses no political threat to the Roman Empire (7:1–10; 23:1–16).

2. Jesus the Prophet

At the start of his public ministry in the synagogue at Nazareth (4:16–30), Jesus declares that the words of Isaiah 61 ("the Spirit of the Lord is upon me") are being fulfilled in his ministry ("today"). He goes on to place himself in line with the great Old Testament prophets, Elijah and Elisha, especially in terms of their prophetic ministries extending beyond the limits of Israel. When Jesus restores to life the son of the widow of Nain, the crowd of witnesses concludes that "a great prophet has risen among us" (7:16). Jesus willingly continues his journey up to Jerusalem on the grounds that "it is impossible for a prophet to be killed outside of Jerusalem" (13:33). During his passion, Jesus is mocked as a prophet (22:64), though his tormentors are ironically correct in their assessment of him. And when the risen Jesus explains to the two disciples on the way to Emmaus why he had to suffer and die, he appeals to what the prophets had to say about the Messiah (24:25–27). At Pentecost, the Spirit of prophecy is granted to the community of Jesus' disciples gathered in Jerusalem (Acts 2:1–4). Luke is as much interested in prophetic succession as he is in apostolic succession.

3. The Twelve Apostles

More than the other Evangelists, Luke is responsible for putting together the words *twelve* and *apostles*. According to 6:13, Jesus "called his disciples and chose twelve of them, whom he also named apostles." Luke then goes on to list them by name: Simon Peter, Andrew, James, John, and so on. According to 9:1–2, Jesus sends out "the twelve" to extend his mission of proclaiming God's kingdom and healing, while on their return "the apostles" in 9:10 tell Jesus all they have done. Throughout the Gospel narrative, there are reminders about the twelve apostles as the closest companions of Jesus (see 11:49; 17:5; 22:14; 24:10). Likewise in Acts, there are many references to the twelve apostles (see 1:2, 26; 2:37, 42–43; 4:33–36; 5:2, 12, 18, 29, 40; etc.). In Luke–Acts the twelve apostles serve as principles of continuity between the time of Jesus and the time of the Holy Spirit. The church has derived the concept of apostolic succession from this theme in the writings of Luke. His generally positive picture of the twelve apostles contrasts rather sharply with their negative portrayal in the second half of Mark's Gospel.

4. Women

In Luke's infancy narrative women such as Elizabeth, Mary, and Anna play prominent roles and represent many of the best features of Old Testament piety. The episode about the sinful woman anointing Jesus in 7:36–50 illustrates the close relationship between love for God and Jesus and the forgiveness of sins. According to 8:1–3, a group of women followers (most prominently, Mary Magdalene) accompanied Jesus and the apostles and contributed greatly to his public ministry. Along the way to Jerusalem, sisters Mary and Martha offer hospitality to Jesus and his companions (10:38–42). Women are featured in Jesus' parables of the lost coin (15:8–10) and the persistent widow (18:1–8). The women disciples at the cross see Jesus die and see where he is buried (23:49, 55). When they go to his tomb on Easter Sunday morning, they find it empty and report that fact to the apostles (24:1–12). While Luke clearly gives special prominence to women, scholars today debate whether he really promotes the cause of women or merely "keeps them in their place" by assigning to them the household tasks conventionally carried out by women in first-century Jewish and Greco-Roman society.

5. Prayer

Luke's Gospel contains two substantial instructions about prayer. In 11:1–13 Jesus responds to his disciples' request for a sample prayer with the shorter version of the Lord's Prayer, and he provides parables and sayings on being persistent in the prayer of petition. In 18:1–14 Jesus again takes up the theme of persistence in prayer with the parable of the persistent widow, and then he contrasts the self-absorbed prayer of the Pharisee with the humble prayer of the tax collector ("God, be merciful to me, a sinner!"). Luke also notes that Jesus prays at decisive moments in his life: his baptism (3:21), the healing of a leper (5:16), the choosing of the twelve apostles (6:12), Peter's confession of him as the Messiah of God (9:18), the Transfiguration (9:28–29), his arrest (22:40–46), and his death (23:34, 46). Several of these prayer accounts highlight Jesus' special relationship with God as his Father. The frequent mention of Jesus at prayer is one reason Luke's Gospel is sometimes described as the Gospel of prayer.

6. Rich and Poor

Relationships between rich and poor persons, and the importance of the rich sharing their goods with the poor in the present, are important themes in Luke's Gospel. Mary's Magnificat prophesies that when the great reversal occurs, God will fill the hungry with good things and send the rich away empty (1:53). This prophecy is enacted graphically in the story of Lazarus and the rich man in 16:19–31, where the challenge is for the rich to share their goods with the poor before it is too late, when there will be a "great chasm" fixed between heaven and Hades. Similar teachings are found in the blessings and woes (6:20–26), the parable of the rich fool (12:13–21), the advice about planning the guest list for a banquet (14:12–14), and the story of Zacchaeus (19:1–10).

7. Banquet

The Old Testament gives special prominence to meals in various contexts. In addition to the normal human fellowship and hospitality that are part of sharing a meal with others, the Bible associates meals with the making of covenants, offering sacrifices, sharing wisdom, and imagining what the fullness of God's kingdom will be like. One of the most certain and controversial aspects of Jesus' public ministry was his practice of sharing meals with such marginal characters as tax collectors and sinners. These meals were intended as previews or anticipations of life's fullness in God's kingdom. Luke's Gospel gives particular attention to banquet scenes:

- the banquet at the house of Simon the Pharisee, where the sinful woman anoints Jesus (7:36–50)
- the feeding of the five thousand (9:10–17)
- the discourse against the Pharisees (11:37–52)
- Jesus' teachings about the kingdom of God (14:1–24)

Once Jesus was asked by the Pharisees when the kingdom of God was coming, and he answered, "The kingdom of God is not coming with things that can be observed; nor will they say, 'Look, here it is!' or 'There it is!' For, in fact, the kingdom of God is among you."

—Luke 17:20–21

- the Last Supper (22:1–38)
- the appearances of the risen Jesus on the road to Emmaus (24:13–35) and in Jerusalem (24:36–49)

These scenes are occasions for Jesus' teachings and for fellowship with him, as well as previews of the banquet that will take place in the fullness of God's kingdom.

8. Eschatology

The word *eschatology* refers to the study (*logos*) of the "last things" (*eschata*). In the world of the New Testament, the last things include the resurrection of the dead, the last judgment, and rewards for the wise and righteous and punishments for the foolish and wicked. In Luke's Gospel (as well as the Gospels of Matthew and Mark) the time of the last things is to be inaugurated by the coming of the Son of Man (see Daniel 7:13–14). Early Christians identified Jesus as the Son of Man and looked forward to his second coming, or *parousia*. According to Luke (and other New Testament writers), the future coming of the Son of Man is certain but its precise timing is indefinite. Therefore the proper attitude for us to have in the present is constant watchfulness or vigilance (Luke 12:35–48). Even though the kingdom of God is already among us (17:20–21), its future fullness will be so sudden and so obvious that the search for preliminary signs will be futile (17:22–37). The events surrounding the coming of the glorious Son of Man (21:5–36) call for patient endurance (21:19). But for the faithful remnant, they are ultimately a cause for joy because they mean that "your redemption is drawing near" (21:28).

9. Jerusalem

Luke's narrative about Jesus begins in the Jerusalem temple with the angel Gabriel's announcement of John's birth (1:5–25). At age twelve Jesus goes with his parents on a pilgrimage to Jerusalem at Passover, and he displays great wisdom among the sages at the Jerusalem temple (2:41–52). When he's an adult, his long journey from Galilee reaches its goal at the Jerusalem temple. He takes possession of the temple area and exercises a substantial ministry there and in the area of Jerusalem (19:45—21:38). After his resurrection, Jesus appears to his followers first on the road from Jerusalem to Emmaus (24:13–35) and then in Jerusalem itself (24:36–49). In commissioning his disciples to proclaim repentance and forgiveness of sins to all nations, the risen Jesus specifies that they begin from Jerusalem. The Acts of the Apostles will trace the spread of the Gospel from Jerusalem (see Acts 1—7) to the ends of the earth, which from an ancient Mediterranean perspective was Rome and Spain (see Acts 27—28).

10. Holy Spirit

According to Luke's infancy narrative, Jesus is conceived through the Holy Spirit (1:35), and Zechariah and Simeon prophesy under the inspiration of the Holy Spirit (1:67; 2:25–35). At Jesus' baptism the Spirit descends upon him (3:21–22), and his public

ministry of teaching and healing is empowered by the coming
of the Holy Spirit upon him (4:18–19). Throughout his public
activity Jesus is the bearer of the Holy Spirit par excellence, and
he promises to send the Spirit to his disciples after his ascension
(24:49). In Acts, the Holy Spirit is the great principle of continuity between the time of Jesus and the time of the church. The
Spirit in turn empowers Peter, Paul, and the other apostles to
carry on and replicate the ministry of Jesus outside the land of
Israel.

For Discussion and Reflection

Choose one of the ten themes in Luke, and look carefully at the
passages mentioned. How would a study of this theme or passage
be valuable to you or to your faith community?

Which of these ten themes were not so obvious to you before
you read this chapter? How might you continue exploring that
theme?

PART FOUR

Luke's Gospel in Christian Life

10

Prayer: *Lectio Divina* and Ignatian Contemplation

The traditional Christian definition of prayer is the lifting of the mind and heart to God. In the Christian tradition, the Scriptures—especially the four Gospels—have often served as starting points for prayer. A serious and respectful reading of Gospel texts can make possible an experience of prayer that involves both mind and heart.

Throughout the centuries many methods for praying with the Gospels have developed. This chapter explains and illustrates two rather simple and well-tested methods that successfully engage both the mind and the heart: *lectio divina* (or "sacred reading") and Ignatian contemplation. These two methods are complementary. A person can, and should, try both approaches and then see what elements prove to be most helpful and fruitful. The goal of both methods is to facilitate growth in personal holiness and in closeness to God, not merely to complete rigidly and successfully the steps in a method. I will illustrate each of the two approaches with reference to a key text from Luke's Gospel: the parable of

the prodigal son for *lectio divina*, and the appearance of the risen
Jesus to his disciples in Jerusalem for Ignatian contemplation.

Lectio Divina: The Parable of the Prodigal Son

The method of the devout reading of the Scriptures known as
lectio divina developed early in the history of monasticism and
has been carried on for many centuries in that context. The goal
was to help monks not only know more perfectly the information
contained in the Scriptures but also to let the Scriptures shape
and nourish their spiritual lives. In recent years, however, *lectio
divina* has been adapted and used successfully in wider commu-
nal and pastoral settings.

The approach to *lectio divina* illustrated in this chapter distin-
guishes four steps:

1. reading the text slowly and reverently (*lectio*)
2. reflecting on what the text might mean for me (or us)
    today (*meditatio*)
3. using the text as a vehicle to pray to God in praise and
    thanksgiving or in petition (*oratio*)
4. discerning what I (or we) should do in response to this
    text (*actio*)

Another older version of *lectio divina* identifies the fourth step as
contemplation—that is, simply savoring the whole experience and
letting it sink into the depths of one's soul. Still another approach
divides the fourth step into three movements: discernment,

deliberation, and action. Applying the concerns of *lectio divina* to the parable of the prodigal son will illustrate the basic nature of the whole approach.

Luke 15:11–32

Then Jesus said, "There was a man who had two sons. The younger of them said to his father, 'Father, give me the share of the property that will belong to me.' So he divided his property between them. A few days later the younger son gathered all he had and traveled to a distant country, and there he squandered his property in dissolute living. When he had spent everything, a severe famine took place throughout that country, and he began to be in need. So he went and hired himself out to one of the citizens of that country, who sent him to his fields to feed the pigs. He would gladly have filled himself with the pods that the pigs were eating; and no one gave him anything. But when he came to himself he said, 'How many of my father's hired hands have bread enough and to spare, but here I am dying of hunger! I will get up and go to my father, and I will say to him, "Father, I have sinned against heaven and before you; I am no longer worthy to be called your son; treat me like one of your hired hands."' So he set off and went to his father. But while he was still far off, his father saw him and was filled with compassion; he ran and put his arms around him and kissed him. Then the son said to him, 'Father, I have sinned against heaven and before you; I am no longer worthy to be called your son.' But the father said to his slaves, 'Quickly, bring out a robe—the best one—and put it on him; put a ring on his finger and sandals on his feet. And get the fatted calf and kill it, and let us eat and celebrate; for this son of mine was dead and is alive again; he was lost and is found!' And they began to celebrate.

"Now his elder son was in the field; and when he came and approached the house, he heard music and dancing. He called one of the slaves and asked what was going on. He replied, 'Your brother has come, and your father has killed the fatted calf, because he has got him back safe and sound.' Then he became angry and refused to go in. His father came out and began to plead with him. But he answered his father, 'Listen! For all these years I have been working like a slave for you, and I have never disobeyed your command; yet you have never given me even a young goat so that I might celebrate with my friends. But when this son of yours came back, who has devoured your property with prostitutes, you killed the fatted calf for him!' Then the father said to him, 'Son, you are always with me, and all that is mine is yours. But we had to celebrate and rejoice, because this brother of yours was dead and has come to life; he was lost and has been found.'"

Step 1: Read the whole text reverently and slowly.

We need to savor the words and images along the way. The initial reading also involves thinking about the passage along the lines developed in our narrative analysis of Luke's Gospel. That is, we need to look at the characters, how they are portrayed, and how they interact with one another. We need also to consider the structure or plot of the story, how the events unfold, and what kind of resolution (if any) is reached at the end. Finally we need to reflect on the purpose of the parable in terms of Jesus' ministry and Luke's Gospel.

The parable of the prodigal son is the third and longest in a set of three parables in Luke 15 about finding what was lost: a lost sheep, a lost coin, and a lost son. In the two short parables first a shepherd and then a woman goes in search of what had been lost, finds it, and rejoices over the finding. The occasion for these parables is the complaint from Pharisees and scribes that Jesus was spending too much time with suspicious figures, such as tax collectors and sinners. In response Jesus uses the three parables to explain and defend his outreach to such characters as reflecting God's own outreach to the lost. His point is that he is doing what God does in offering all of us the possibility of forgiveness of sins and of reconciliation with God.

The parable of the prodigal son has two main parts, one featuring the younger or "prodigal" son (15:11–24), and the other featuring the older son (15:25–32). The younger son demands his share of the inheritance, goes off to a distant country, and squanders all his money. Reduced to the degrading task of feeding pigs, the prodigal (in the negative sense of being wasteful) comes to his senses and determines to return home in the hope that his father will accept him as a hired servant. What is most surprising is that when the father catches sight of his son returning, he runs out to meet him, kisses him, accepts his apology, and organizes a great celebration. The father is prodigal in the positive sense of being lavishly generous, despite the injustice committed by the son.

The part about the older son addresses the situation of pious and observant persons (Pharisees and scribes) who are offended by Jesus' offers of repentance and forgiveness to such disreputable persons as tax collectors and sinners. The elder son complains about the apparent injustice involved in his father's acceptance and forgiveness of the younger son while not rewarding his own years of faithful service. He refuses to join the celebration and addresses his father in a disrespectful manner ("Listen!"). In response the father is polite ("Son") and insists that "we had to celebrate and rejoice" because the brother who had been lost and as good as dead was now found and alive and well.

We are not told how the elder son reacted. He may have remained adamant in his anger. Or he may have accepted his father's explanation and joined in the celebration. The ending is left open. So also it was up to the grumbling Pharisees and scribes to accept or reject Jesus' defense of God's mercy to sinners and his own ministry to marginal persons.

Step 2: Reflect on what the text might mean for you today.

Meditatio on the parable of the prodigal son might go in various directions. You could focus on the story as an example of the biblical dynamic of sin, repentance, and forgiveness. Sin involves turning aside from God and God's commands. Nevertheless, God patiently and lovingly awaits our repentance and return. For us, repentance means acknowledging our sins and throwing ourselves on God's mercy. Forgiveness and reconciliation are possible only because of God's mercy.

Another approach to meditation would be to look at the three main characters in the parable and to discern where you are in your own life. You might best identify with the prodigal son because at this point you find yourself feeling sinful. The issue might be addictive behavior or meanness of spirit or loss of hope. The prodigal son reminds us that we can acknowledge our sinfulness, cast ourselves on God's mercy, and be reconciled to God and to those we may have offended. Or you might identify with the elder son because you find yourself resenting the "easy" conversions of others or are jealous of others because of their success. Or you might identify with the father. Perhaps there are tensions in your own family or community. Is there anyone who has done something to you that you cannot forgive? Is there anything you have done that has caused a split between others? Is there something you can do to repair that damage now? Can you summon up the greatness of spirit that the father showed to both sons?

Step 3: Use the text to guide your prayer.

How you pray (*oratio*) as the result of reading this passage depends on which direction your meditation has taken you. You might want to praise God for your own experience of being forgiven and reconciled to God. Or you might pray for someone dear to you who seems unable to get free from sin. You might give thanks to

God for someone who has turned his or her life around. Or you might ask for wisdom and courage in trying to reconcile family members or friends to one another and to God.

Step 4: Discern how to respond to the text through action. What you might do (*actio*) also flows from your meditation and prayer. You might decide to go to confession and seek sacramental reconciliation with God. Or you might plan and participate in an intervention in the hope of helping someone get his or her life back on track. You might let go of your resentment toward someone who has offended or harmed you and do something positive to restore your relationship.

Ignatian Contemplation: The Appearance of the Risen Jesus to His Disciples in Jerusalem

The approach to reading and praying over the Gospels known as Ignatian contemplation derives from the Spiritual Exercises of St. Ignatius of Loyola, the sixteenth-century founder of the Society of Jesus (Jesuits). His written *Spiritual Exercises* was intended as a practical manual for those directing an Ignatian formation experience, often with the goal of helping the retreatant or exercitant come to a decision about choosing a state in life or making some other major decision. As noted above, this method should be viewed not as a rival or alternative to *lectio divina*, but rather as a development and refinement of it. It involves reading, meditating on, praying over, and applying Gospel passages and other biblical texts.

A major component of Ignatius's Spiritual Exercises is the contemplation of Gospel texts. In the course of these contemplations the four basic questions that arise in *lectio divina* also come to the surface:

1. What does this Gospel passage say?
2. What does it say to me here and now?
3. What do I want to say to God on the basis of this text?
4. What must I do in response to my experience of God in this text?

The most distinctive feature of Ignatian contemplation is the use of the imagination with the Gospel text. Ignatius urges the retreatant to imagine himself or herself as a spectator or even a participant in the Gospel scene. He urges us to apply our senses to the scene and to ask and answer some basic questions: What do I see? What do I hear? What do I smell? What might I taste? and What might I touch? He wants us to focus on the various characters and to identify with their actions and reactions. We can illustrate Ignatius's way of reading and applying Gospel texts by applying these questions and imaginative practices to Luke's account of the risen Jesus appearing to his disciples gathered in Jerusalem.

Luke 24:36–49
While they were talking about this, Jesus himself stood among them and said to them, "Peace be with

you." They were startled and terrified, and thought that they were seeing a ghost. He said to them, "Why are you frightened, and why do doubts arise in your hearts? Look at my hands and my feet; see that it is I myself. Touch me and see; for a ghost does not have flesh and bones as you see that I have." And when he had said this, he showed them his hands and his feet. While in their joy they were disbelieving and still wondering, he said to them, "Have you anything here to eat?" They gave him a piece of broiled fish, and he took it and ate in their presence.

Then he said to them, "These are my words that I spoke to you while I was still with you—that everything written about me in the law of Moses, the prophets, and the psalms must be fulfilled." Then he opened their minds to understand the scriptures, and he said to them, "Thus it is written, that the Messiah is to suffer and to rise from the dead on the third day, and that repentance and forgiveness of sins is to be proclaimed in his name to all nations, beginning from Jerusalem. You are witnesses of these things. And see, I am sending upon you what my Father promised; so stay here in the city until you have been clothed with power from on high."

Ignatian contemplation presupposes the slow and reverent reading of the biblical passage, as well as attention to the basic concerns of literary criticism: words and images, characters, plot or structure, literary form, and message. In addition to reading the text intelligently and thoughtfully, a person following Ignatian practice will participate in the biblical scene by way of the imagination.

Luke 24 contains two relatively long accounts of appearances of the risen Jesus to his followers: to the two disciples on their way to Emmaus (24:13–35) and to the eleven apostles and their companions in Jerusalem (24:36–49). In both cases Jesus opens up the Scriptures to show why he had to suffer and die, and he shares a meal with them as proof that he is more than a ghost or disembodied spirit. In the first account the Scriptures come first and then the meal, while in the second passage the sequence is the meal first and then the Scriptures.

The second appearance takes place in Jerusalem while the apostles and their companions are already sharing a meal. They had heard that the women found Jesus' tomb empty, and Peter verified their report (24:10–12). Nevertheless, the empty tomb was not absolute proof that Jesus had been raised from the dead. What they needed was a personal experience of the risen Jesus.

The meal section of the second appearance story lends itself well to the application of the senses and Ignatian contemplation. Imagine yourself as one of the companions of the eleven apostles (minus Judas, of course). The risen Jesus suddenly appears, identifies himself, and shows that he is not a ghost by eating a piece of fish. Ask yourself, What do I see? What does the risen Jesus look like? What is he wearing? What impression does he make on the apostles? What impression does he make on you?

Next ask yourself, What do I hear? What is Jesus' tone of voice? Is it soothing ("peace") or edgy (since the apostles had recently deserted him)? What effects do his words have on them? What effects do they have on you? Do you dare to touch his hands and feet? What impression does that make on you? Can you smell the odor of the cooked fish? Have you eaten some yourself? What does Jesus eating the fish prove? How do you come away from the whole sensuous experience? Do you now believe that Jesus has really been raised from the dead?

The point of all these questions is to get you as a reader to participate in the biblical scene by exercising the power of your imagination. Each of us will have different images and perspectives. However, the effect of applying our senses is to bring to life scenes that we now know only through reading the words on the page.

The second part of the Jerusalem appearance scene consists of a Scripture lesson and a commission. The risen Jesus first explains that his passion, death, and resurrection took place according to God's will as revealed in Israel's Scriptures. Then he commissions the apostles to preach the good news of repentance and forgiveness in his name "to all nations, beginning from Jerusalem" (24:47). But before that, they must wait for the gift of the Holy Spirit to be bestowed on them at Pentecost (see Acts 2).

The scene at the meal remains the same. But now attention is almost entirely on what Jesus says. How do you imagine the tone of his voice? Is it calming or exasperated? What Scriptures does he refer to? What might his commission mean for the apostles and for you? Where do his assurances leave you emotionally? Can you chart the course of your emotions from start to finish?

Meditation on Luke 24:36–49 might focus on its many rich theological themes: Jesus' resurrection as the basis of our own hope for resurrection, Jesus as the fulfillment of Israel's Scriptures, and mission as the proper response to encountering the risen Jesus. However, the application of the senses and the participatory approach encouraged by Ignatian contemplation might also lead you to place more emphasis on the emotional dimensions involved in reading and meditating on this text.

Using your imagination, you might reflect on the mood swings that the apostles and you have experienced during this encounter: disappointment and gloom over Jesus' death, confusion at the report that his tomb was found empty, being startled by his sudden reappearance, guilt over having betrayed him, joy at experiencing his presence once more, amazement that a dead person could now be alive, recognition that all had taken place in accord with the Scriptures, and eagerness to tell the good news to others, even "all nations."

In praying on Luke 24:36–49 you may want to thank God for the gift of faith in the risen Jesus and to ask God to deepen and strengthen that faith. Or you may seek the guidance of the Holy Spirit in order to discern how you might best share the good news of the risen Jesus with others. You may ask God to make you a more positive and hopeful person, one who trusts God to bring good out of even the most unlikely and apparently hopeless situations.

Again, the action that you might decide upon will flow from your meditation and prayer. On the basis of Luke 24:36–49, you could decide to read the Old Testament Scriptures on a more regular basis. Or you could participate in, or contribute to, a Christian missionary outreach at home or abroad. You could determine to examine your conscience every day, and see whether in daily life your faith in the risen Jesus really affects who you are and what you do.

The methods of *lectio divina* and Ignatian contemplation are simple and proven ways to approach the Gospels and other biblical texts. They make it possible to integrate serious academic study of Scripture with the desires and needs of the human spirit. Once you have worked with these methods or some combination of them over time, you can then determine what approach to Scripture best fits your talents, needs, and hopes.

For Reflection and Discussion

Apply the four steps of *lectio divina* to another text in Luke, such as 5:1–11; 9:28–36; 19:1–10; or 23:44–49.

Apply the approach of Ignatian contemplation to the other resurrection appearance story in Luke 24:13–35 or to any of the texts listed above.

What positive values do you find in these approaches to Scripture?

11

The Actualization of Scripture and Christian Life

The term *actualization* refers to bringing the significance of Scripture into the present. The most obvious way of actualization is through prayer according to the methods of *lectio divina* and Ignatian contemplation outlined in the preceding chapter. Other forms of actualizing Scripture include Bible study groups, the homily or sermon, and artistic or dramatic presentations of biblical passages or themes.

Luke's Gospel provides an especially rich opportunity for the actualization of Scripture. Its literary artistry makes it an attractive book, and its theological simplicity and profundity provide many challenges along the way. Its emphasis on Jesus' life as the best example of his own teaching calls us to follow his lead and to "go and do likewise." The challenge of Luke's Gospel is especially apparent in Year C in the lectionary of Sunday Scripture readings for Mass, where there is an abundance of selections from Luke's Gospel.

The Year of St. Luke in the Church's Lectionary

In response to a directive from the Second Vatican Council (1962–65), the Catholic Church adopted in the early 1970s a three-year Sunday lectionary and a two-year daily lectionary for its Scripture readings. Many mainline Protestant churches followed and adapted the Catholic lectionary to their traditions and needs.

For each year, on Sundays one of the first three (synoptic) Gospels serves as the lead text: Matthew for Year A, Mark for Year B, and Luke for Year C. Selections from John's Gospel appear in each cycle, especially around Christmas, during Lent, and in the Easter season. The Old Testament reading and the responsorial psalm are usually chosen for their thematic relationship to the Gospel reading. The readings from Paul's letters or from other New Testament epistles represent a separate cycle, though there are sometimes thematic links to the other readings.

On weekdays, the first reading is from the Old Testament or from New Testament books other than the Gospels, and the Psalm shows some relation to it. In Ordinary Time there are continuous readings each year from the Gospels of Mark, Matthew, and Luke, in turn. During Lent and the Easter season there are many selections from John's Gospel. Thus over the years Catholics and other Christians are exposed to much of the New Testament and large parts of the Old Testament.

In the Year C (2010, 2013, 2016, etc.), most of the Sunday Gospel readings are from Luke's Gospel. The appendix on pp. 131–132 lists the passages from Luke that are read on the Sundays in Ordinary Time and the seasons of Advent, Christmas, Lent, and Easter. The list illustrates why the Year C in the lectionary cycle is often referred to as the Year of Luke.

The Lucan passages for the thirty-four Sundays in Ordinary Time trace Jesus' words and deeds through the course of his baptism and public ministry from his inaugural discourse in the synagogue in Nazareth to his final discourse in Jerusalem. The Advent Sunday readings from Luke take one passage from the final discourse, then focus on John the Baptist and recount the events leading up to Jesus' birth. The pertinent passages from Luke's infancy narrative provide the basic story line for the Christmas season. During Lent the Lucan temptation and Transfiguration texts are read, as well as a passage about repentance and the parable of the prodigal son. The Passion narrative according to Luke is read on Palm Sunday, and Lucan texts are used on Easter Sunday and at the Ascension.

The church's lectionary offers preachers and teachers a precious opportunity. The principle of continuous reading makes it possible to stand beside the individual Evangelists, each in turn, and to grow in appreciation of their distinctive literary artistry and theological insights. As we have seen, Luke communicates mainly through narratives that are carefully constructed and give unity to his story of Jesus by developing themes that run through the whole Gospel and spill over into the Acts of the Apostles. The major characters that Luke portrays over the course of his narrative—Jesus and the apostles—interact with equally memorable characters who are on stage for only a short time—Elizabeth and Zechariah, John the Baptist, Mary, Zacchaeus, Pontius Pilate, Herod Antipas, and the Emmaus pilgrims.

There is also in Luke's Gospel a subtle simplicity. What sometimes looks straightforward and easy to understand often under further review can seem more complex and sophisticated than it might appear at first sight. Like many other great writers, Luke stimulates us to go beyond surface impressions and to think more deeply about what he has written.

Jesus as the Center of Luke's Theology

When Luke came to write his Gospel, he had access to an already rich tradition about Jesus. From Mark he knew about Jesus as a powerful healer, an authoritative teacher, and a suffering Messiah. From Q he had a collection of Jesus' sayings that illustrated his wisdom. From the special source(s) labeled L he could present traditions associated with the birth of Jesus and some of his most memorable teachings, such as the parables of the Good Samaritan and the prodigal son. From Paul and even the pre-Pauline tradition Luke became familiar with the titles applied to Jesus by the earliest Christians: Messiah or Christ, Son of David, Son of Man, Son of God, and Lord.

While integrating all these sources and traditions into his narrative about Jesus, Luke also developed his own distinctive portrait of Jesus. In Luke's schema of salvation history Jesus stands at the center between the time of Israel and the time of the Holy Spirit (or the church). It is as if all the energy of the Holy Spirit was focused on Jesus, and only after his ascension was this energy to be poured out on the community of Jesus' followers at Pentecost.

The community of Jesus' followers is rooted in the apostles and other disciples called by him during his earthly ministry. Women such as Mary Magdalene (see 8:1–3) were witnesses to Jesus' wise teachings, powerful healings, and passion, death, and resurrection. They all shared meals with Jesus, meals that anticipated his last supper and the banquet to be celebrated fully in the kingdom of God.

The Jesus of Luke's Gospel teaches his disciples what to pray (the Lord's Prayer) and how to pray (with boldness and persistence). He urges his wealthy followers to share their possessions with the poor before it is too late and to divest themselves of whatever might be an obstacle to discipleship and entering the kingdom of God.

While pointing to the presence of God's kingdom in his own ministry ("today"), the Lucan Jesus also insists on the future fullness of that kingdom and warns his followers to be prepared always for God's final judgment and to view it not as something to be feared but rather as the occasion of their vindication and redemption. From birth to death, the Lucan Jesus lives and works in the Holy Land and against the background of Israel's Scriptures and his Jewish heritage. At the same time, what the Lucan Jesus does and teaches prepares the way for the spread of the gospel beyond the geographical limits of Israel and the ethnic boundaries of the Jewish people.

Among Luke's most important contributions to our understanding of Jesus are his portrayals of him as a prophet, martyr or witness, and good example. As a prophet Jesus stands in line with Elijah and Elisha, is acknowledged by the people as "a great prophet" (7:16), and speaks God's word to his people. The Lucan Jesus also bears witness to God as his Father and goes to his death as a faithful witness to his own best teachings. And he offers a good example as the champion of marginal persons, as compassionate to those in need, and as one who practices what he preaches.

Some of Luke's most precious insights about Jesus come together in Luke's account of Jesus' death in 23:44–49. The homily that follows reflects on this text and represents an attempt to highlight those insights and to suggest what they can mean for us today (actualization). It gives particular attention to Jesus' last words (taken from Psalm 31:5) according to Luke 23:46: "Father, into your hands I commend my spirit."

Luke 23:44–49

It was now about noon, and darkness came over the whole land until three in the afternoon, while the sun's light failed; and the curtain of the temple was torn in two. Then Jesus, crying with a loud voice, said, "Father, into your hands I commend my spirit." Having said this, he breathed his last. When the centurion saw what had taken place, he praised God and said, "Certainly this man was innocent." And when all the crowds who had gathered there for this spectacle saw what had taken place, they returned home, beating their breasts. But all his acquaintances, including the women who had followed him from Galilee, stood at a distance, watching these things.

Homily Based on Luke's Account of Jesus' Death

"Father, into your hands I commend my spirit." In Luke's Gospel, Jesus speaks three times while hanging on the cross. In each case the dying Jesus shows himself faithful to the principles that he taught during his public ministry. First, in Luke 23:34 Jesus asks his heavenly Father to forgive his enemies, and so he practices his own principle of loving our enemies. Then in 23:43 Jesus promises the "good thief" a place in paradise, and so even on the cross Jesus continues his ministry to marginal persons. Up to the very end, Jesus practices what he preaches, is true to his own principles, and offers us a worthy example.

In the third and final saying according to Luke (23:46), Jesus says, "Father, into your hands I commend my spirit." With these words Jesus makes his own the words of Psalm 31:5, one of the Old Testament lament psalms. These are the words of an innocent sufferer, of one who trusts God totally and who hopes for vindication from God.

Jesus is an innocent sufferer. All four Gospels emphasize the fundamental innocence of Jesus. The charges against him are trumped up. The witnesses are liars. The officials are corrupt. And yet the legal process against Jesus moves inexorably forward. Psalm 31 is the prayer of an innocent sufferer. The psalmist says that "they scheme together against me, as they plot to take my life" (verse 13). Thus the psalmist and Jesus stand in solidarity with all other innocent sufferers of the past and present.

Jesus trusts God totally. The apostles have deserted him. He is undergoing a cruel punishment that will surely end with his death. And yet Jesus prays to God as his heavenly Father. According to Luke, Jesus prays at the most important moments throughout his ministry: his baptism, his choice of the twelve apostles, Peter's confession of him as the Messiah, his transfiguration, his agony in the garden, and so on. And invariably these accounts of Jesus at prayer allude to his identity as the Son of God and his relationship to God as his Father. Indeed, Jesus teaches us all to address God as "Father" after his own example. Throughout his public ministry Jesus teaches others to trust in God. He declares as "blessed" the poor, the hungry, and the weeping. He teaches us not to be anxious about what we are to eat or to wear, because the Father has been pleased to give us his kingdom. Here at the moment of his death Jesus shows perfect trust in God. He hands over his very self to his heavenly Father.

Jesus hopes for vindication from God. The words of Psalm 31 read in their entirety are the words of someone who fully expects that God will vindicate him. The psalmist proclaims God to be his rock of refuge and his strong fortress, prays ardently for rescue from his enemies, and affirms that "the Lord preserves the faithful" (Psalm 31:23). These are not the words of a defeated and despairing person. Rather, they are the words of a trusting and hopeful person. All along, Jesus has taught people to look for the vindication of the wise and righteous when God's kingdom comes in its fullness. Then the poor, the hungry, and the weeping will share in the overwhelming joy of God's kingdom.

Then the lowly will be raised up, and the high and mighty will be put down.

The story of Jesus does not end with his death on Good Friday but moves forward to his resurrection on Easter Sunday. The resurrection of Jesus is the vindication of all his life, teaching, healing, and suffering. He trusted God, and God vindicated him. He hoped in God, and God gave him life again. His resurrection is the basis for *our* hope in eternal life with God.

"Father, into your hands I commend my spirit." With these final words, Jesus once more practices what he preaches, remains true to his own principles, and offers us an example. These are the words of an innocent sufferer, of one who trusts God totally, and of one who hopes for vindication from God. They can and should be our words too. Amen.

"Go and Do Likewise"

One of the most famous and beloved texts in Luke's Gospel is the parable of the Good Samaritan (10:25–37). When a lawyer asks Jesus "Who is my neighbor?" Jesus tells the story of a man who was beaten, robbed, and left for dead on the road between Jerusalem and Jericho. The injured man receives no help from a priest or from a Levite. The one who does help him is a Samaritan, someone whose identity as a Jew was suspect. When the lawyer is pressed to answer his own question and to admit that it was the Samaritan who showed himself to be the injured man's neighbor, Jesus challenges him (and us) to "go and do likewise."

As we have seen, Luke's Jesus is the best example of his own teachings. The challenge of Luke's Gospel is for us to imitate Jesus' example and "go and do likewise." Throughout his Gospel, Luke portrays Jesus as the pattern or model for Christians. This insight is developed especially in Luke's portrayal of Paul in the Acts of the Apostles. In this development Luke may have been influenced by the idea of parallel lives made famous by Plutarch. And he may also be echoing Paul's own words, "Be imitators of me, as I am of Christ" (1 Corinthians 11:1).

The most striking parallels between Jesus in Luke's Gospel and Paul in Acts include the following:

the prophecies about their significance for Gentiles and about their sufferings	Luke 2:29–32	Acts 9:15–16
the prefaces to their ministries delivered in synagogues	Luke 4:16–30	Acts 13:14–52
their determination to go up to Jerusalem despite the sufferings that it may bring upon them	Luke 9:51	Acts 19:21
their detailed Passion predictions	Luke 9:22, 44–45	Acts 20:22–24; 21:10–14
their farewell speeches	Luke 22:21–38	Acts 20:18–35
their heroism in accepting a martyr's death	Luke 22:39–46	Acts 21:12–14
their trial narratives	Luke 22:47—23:25	Acts 21:27—26:32

Thus Luke develops continuity between the lives of Jesus and Paul, and the example of Jesus provides the pattern not only for Paul's life but also for the lives of all Christians. The message of Luke's two-volume work as a whole is best summarized in Jesus' own words to the lawyer, "Go and do likewise."

For Reflection and Discussion

What aspects of Luke's Gospel do you find most attractive?

What aspects do you find most difficult or challenging?

How has your reading of Luke's Gospel enriched your appreciation of Jesus and of the Evangelist?

Readings from Luke's Gospel for the Sundays and Feasts in the Year C

Sundays in Ordinary Time
1. 3:15–16, 21–22
3. 1:1–4; 4:14–21
4. 4:21–30
5. 5:1–11
6. 5:17, 20–26
7. 6:27–38
8. 6:39–45
9. 7:7–10
10. 7:11–17
11. 7:36—8:3
12. 9:18–24
13. 9:51–62
14. 10:1–12, 17–20
15. 10:25–37
16. 10:38–42
17. 11:1–13
18. 12:13–21
19. 12:32–48
20. 12:49–53
21. 13:22–30
22. 14:1, 7–14

23. 14:25–33
24. 15:1–32
25. 16:1–13
26. 16:19–31
27. 17:5–10
28. 17:11–19
29. 18:1–8
30. 18:9–14
31. 19:1–10
32. 20:27–38
33. 21:5–13
34. 23:35–43

Advent and Christmas
1. 21:25–28, 34–36
2. 3:1–6
3. 3:10–18
4. 1:39–45
Immaculate Conception
    1:26–38
Christmas: Midnight 2:1–14
Christmas: Dawn 2:15–20

Holy Family 2:41–52

Mary the Mother of God
  2:16–21

Presentation 2:21–40

Lent and Easter

1. 4:1–13

2. 9:28–36

3. 13:1–9

4. 15:1–3, 11–32

5. Palm Sunday
  22:14—23:56

6. Easter 24:1–12; 24:13–35

7. Ascension 24:46–53

For Further Reading

Bovon, François. *Luke*. Minneapolis: Fortress, 2002.

———. *Luke the Theologian*. Waco, TX: Baylor University Press, 2006.

Byrne, Brendan. *The Hospitality of God*. Collegeville, MN: Liturgical Press, 2000.

Conzelmann, Hans. *The Theology of St. Luke*. Philadelphia: Fortress, 1960.

Esler, Philip F. *Community and Gospel in Luke–Acts*. Cambridge: Cambridge University Press, 1987.

Fitzmyer, Joseph A. *The Gospel according to Luke*. New York: Doubleday, 1981, 1985.

———. *Luke the Theologian*. New York: Paulist, 1989.

Johnson, Luke Timothy. *The Gospel of Luke*. Collegeville, MN: Liturgical Press, 1991.

O'Toole, Robert F. *Luke's Presentation of Jesus*. Rome: Biblical Institute Press, 2004.

Tannehill, Robert C. *Luke*. Nashville: Abingdon, 1996.

About the Author

Daniel J. Harrington, SJ, is professor of New Testament at Boston College School of Theology and Ministry. He wrote "The Word" column for *America* magazine from 2005 to 2008. He has been writing an annual survey of recent "Books on the Bible" for *America* since 1984.

Harrington has been editor of New Testament Abstracts since 1972 and served as president of the Catholic Biblical Association in 1985–86. He was a member of the official team for editing the Dead Sea Scrolls and focused on the wisdom texts from Qumran. He is also the editor of the Sacra Pagina commentary on the New Testament (Liturgical Press) to which he contributed the volumes on Matthew, Mark (with John Donahue), and 1 & 2 Peter and Jude (with Donald Senior). He has published extensively on the New Testament and on Second Temple Judaism.